Future Psychoanalysis

Future Psychoanalysis

Toward a Psychology of the Human Subject

Ahmed Fayek

LEXINGTON BOOKS
Lanham • Boulder • New York • London

Published by Lexington Books
An imprint of The Rowman & Littlefield Publishing Group, Inc.
4501 Forbes Boulevard, Suite 200, Lanham, Maryland 20706
www.rowman.com

Unit A, Whitacre Mews, 26-34 Stannary Street, London SE11 4AB

British Library Cataloguing in Publication Information Available

Library of Congress Control Number: 2015943428
ISBN: 978-1-4985-2594-7 (cloth: alk. paper)
ISBN: 978-1-4985-2595-4 (ebook)

∞ ™ The paper used in this publication meets the minimum requirements of American National Standard for Information Sciences Permanence of Paper for Printed Library Materials, ANSI/NISO Z39.48-1992.

Printed in the United States of America

Psychoanalysts in the past used to have answers to almost everything about the individual. Psychoanalysts in the future will have many questions about the human subject.

Contents

Preface

Seventy thousand years ago man cognized that he lives in a world of things that happen because of causes (Harari 2014). He accrued a vast amount of information about what causes certain things to happen. Human consciousness emerged and a cognitive revolution was born. After tens of thousands of years, the same man realized that there are unexplainable things and there must be hidden causes for them. Personal beliefs of unseen causes gave birth to animism as the solution to the unseen forces. Seven thousand years ago personal beliefs turned into social convictions, hence the birth of organized religions. Religions were used to answer many questions about causes and effects, and strangely they were able to provide convincing answers to people from then and until now. A few more thousands of years passed before Thales of Mellitus (Johnson 2003) asked questions about knowledge itself and how we could be sure of its correctness, and there philosophy came.

Man did not ask questions about himself. With the birth of philosophy his nature has become subject of curiosity. The first thing that twist in thinking created was distinguishing a difference between subjectivity and objectivity, absolute and relative, and made up the terms that pertain to them. Greek philosophers began to have their say and to be listened to alongside the Oracle readers of Delphi. Yet, it was not possible to know something about man that had not already been a topic of religion. Everything man wanted to know about himself had to be within religious boundaries, in accordance with the religious creed, and never to exceed the dogma of what God permitted and accepted. Man in religion was an issue of morality because he was expected to choose the rightful understandings and explanations given to him about the causes and their effects. Therefore, morality has become an intrinsic part of his cognition. Even when the scientific revolution challenged religion and claimed the independence of knowledge, man remained a moral subject in the sense that he was expected to seek what is right in science. There was reason to keep this attribute cardinal in defining man because he was always seen as the animal with will, thus he had the responsibility of knowing the difference between right and wrong. For five hundred years man's morality—in one way or the other—was the backdrop of any knowledge of man.

In 1900 Freud dissipated this myth by proving that human morality has to be interpreted beyond free will, because man is not free to use his will as he is presumed. Not only because Freud proved that man is not conscious of all of his intentions, but because his will—that is his conscious will—is originally not totally his. It originates in a different period of his life than the one it is called upon, and is formed by a different psychical process than the one he uses to execute. Freud created a major rift in the philosophy of man as subject matter. There came the *individual* whom we thought we knew, followed by the human subject whom we face now with our unfamiliarity. Freud gathered all what could be known about the individual who does not know everything about himself. He postulated an informative theory of a newly discovered individual. It was mainly a theory rich in functional explanations about the individual's attributes. However, his theory revealed an underlying structural base that deals with the human subject, whose morality is not one of his features but one of his dilemmas.

Psychoanalytic literature agrees, in general, that psychoanalysis is stuck and looks like it is in a crisis which could be its end. However, analysts are not trying to articulate the psychoanalytic structural theory and look for a different psychoanalysis based on non-functional conceptions. An attempt of that kind is different from what the contemporary schools have and are still trying to do. They are trying to replace current psychoanalysis with other functional theories. What is needed is to bring out the structural base of psychoanalysis by thoroughly examining the failings of the original functional (informative) theory, so we can agree on the logic of taking the structural theory as future psychoanalysis. The structural theory will confront us with the fact that psychoanalysts cannot do without inputs from a wide range of human scientists who are also in need of structural theories of their own. I tried to extract from the Freudian text what could become a foundation of its structural theory.

Freud's informative theory (his functional conception of man) reached its final destination few decades ago, and is not offering new knowledge of the individual anymore. It exhausted its potentials. Its structural base is beckoning psychoanalysts to move beyond functional thinking. The present theory of psychoanalysis has a glorious past but no future; nevertheless it could give birth to future psychoanalysis.

Introduction

I am introducing in this book an idea which has an explicit background but had no clear foundation until now. The idea is that psychoanalysis, as it stands now, does not seem to have a future, though there are indications that it is not yet finished. The background for this idea is the current situation in psychoanalysis, which is characterized by a daunting crisis that started to peak in the last few decades, with continuing unsuccessful attempts at dealing with it. Those attempts resulted in producing new and different theories of the psyche, which all failed to deal with the crisis that is threatening this great subject called "psychoanalysis." The several attempts at energizing psychoanalysis give the impression that each dealt with a central problem in the matter, considered by some the cause of the crisis. However, reviewing those attempts uncovers the complexity of the problem of psychoanalysis. The continuing and enduring crisis comprises overlapping historical, theoretical, and organizational issues.

The two most pressing aspects of the crisis at the present time are the proliferation of the theories of psychoanalysis, and the declining interest in it by both patients and the young professionals who should be seeking training. The proliferation of theories makes it difficult to know anymore what psychoanalysis is (Fayek 2010), and where can we trace the classical theory in the contemporary theories in order to still call them psychoanalytic. The second aspect of the crisis is multifaceted and warrants special preparations to address.

However serious the problem is now, it should be said that those two aspects were always a concern in the history of psychoanalysis from its very beginning, be it in different forms. The concerns about the purity of the theory caused continuous parting and splitting from the so-called "Freudian classical theory." In the first generation of psychoanalysts the splits were quickly declared and the departing happened with less acrimony, as in the cases of Jung, Stekle, and Adler. Some problems with the same generation of analysts were kept controlled for a while, but eventually came out as it happened with Rank and Ferenczi. At that time—as we will see a little later—those splits were kept under control by the existence of a "Secrete Committee," which was replaced with the organized International Training Committee of the IPA. In the next generation of psychoanalysts, the deviations from the classical theory were looked upon as merely disagreements or personal stands from the basic theory (Alexander, M. Klein, Hartmann, and a few gifted new analysts like Winnicott, Bion, Lacan, and Laplanche). The disagreements in that generation were contained by the loyalty to the Psychoanalytic Institution. The Institution by then, just after Freud's death, was representing the authority of the *profession* of psychoanalysis. This is one of the first and confusing overlaps that contributed to the present crisis of psychoanalysis. Protecting the theory from deviations overlapped with defending the profession from the uninitiated by the training committees, which were stated as the official function of the psychoanalytic institution. Therefore, any attempt at confronting the crisis of psychoanalysis had to deal with the fusion of those two functions of the international organization, which was never done and still seems to puzzle psychoanalysts. The third generation of psychoanalysts had a different way of rebelling against the Freudian doctrine. They came up with pertinent criticisms of some aspects of the theory but showed haste in discarding certain parts of the classical theory, like the concepts of instinct (*Trieb*), and metapsychology. By discarding aspects of the classical theory, they overvalued other aspects they kept and developed to make them look like the entire basis of the theory of psychoanalysis. However, some gifted analysts of the third generation brought forward aspects of psychoanalysis that were part of the original theory but mostly unnoticeable (G. Klein 1976; Green 1977; Hartmann 1964; Lacan 1977b; Laplanche 1997; Winnicott 1955). The third generation made major fundamental changes to the main body of the theory of psychoanalysis by judging some of its information to be irrelevant, considering others to be in need of reconfiguration, and elevating some to the status of the most significant (Brenner 2000). They treated the classical theory as a deficient *informative* theory (a theory that delivers information about the subject matter), thus allowing themselves to reassess the significant conception in that theory.

The theory of psychoanalysis, until the 1970s, was a cohesive theory that one could not dismiss some of its content and keep the others without being obliged to show that the changes do not affect its core premise. Lacan's emphasis and variations on the Oedipus theme brought to the center of attention the significance of that structure in the emergence of the other in the psychical life of the subject. In this way, what was discarded of the theory was reconfigured to integrate in the newly highlighted issues. One could only bypass an older configuration of a certain period of the evolution of the theory as long as another of its newer configuration was made to *substitute* for it (accept the tripartite conception of *ego–super ego–id* to substitute for the tripartite topographical conception of *Cs., Pcs.,* and *Ucs.*). However, metapsychology as a core conception remained as requisite. The third generation analysts' unease with the theory uncovered a major division within the psychoanalytic school of thought. It became clear that the arguments between analysts confuse the information that constitutes their analytical knowledge and the analytic way of thinking that goes beyond the "facts," thus forming a different layer of the theoretical framework; figuratively speaking a deeper layer. Some of the theoretical aspects they brought forward for discussion belonged to the body of information regarding the *psyche* (intrapsychical/interrelational, Ego/Self, etc.). Other aspects pertained mainly to the attitude toward the implementation of psychoanalysis (clinical/theoretical, fixed protocol/changing method of practice, etc.). The distinction made between psychoanalytic information and psychoanalytic implementation was the precursor of other distinctions to be made between the informative theory and the structural theory, the deductive and inductive ways of thinking in analysis, the metapsychology of the individual, and the psychology of the subject. The third generation was the last to hold onto psychoanalysis as school of thought despite their fundamental scrutiny of its main premises. The fourth generation had the road paved to a free-for-all extemporizing of ideas. The reason is that the division uncovered by the third generation revealed that psychoanalysis had come to a point where it had either outgrown its theory or it reached its limits. There was an open invitation to let go of old psychoanalysis and create a new psychoanalysis, or do away with it as a whole. Analysts of the fourth generation clearly showed serious lack of knowledge or understanding of Freud's continuous changes, revisions, and restating of his points of view, which I will come to in chapter 1 in more detail. For instance, Freud doctrine is about the psychodynamics of the intrapsychical structure of the individual, which was his unchanged direction in developing the theory. In the meantime, M. Klein's main contribution to psychoanalysis is revealing and explaining the formation of the intrapsychical in infancy and childhood in the manner we see those formation enacted in interpersonal relationships in adulthood and in transference in particular. Thus, a major mistake of some analysts of the fourth generation was changing psychoanalysis from a theory of the intrapsychical into a theory of interpersonal relationships, without noticing that the latter is built on the former. They took the liberty of *replacing the whole content of the theory with poorly formed variations on the weakest of the third generation so-called innovations* (self-psychology, intersubjectivity, object relations, and extra-psychoanalytic conceptions like neutrality and authority).

The changes made to the theory by the fourth generation of psychoanalysts were radical and to its basic tenets, making it unmistakably another totally different informative theory. They kept almost nothing of the classical psychoanalytic theory in place. Nonetheless, contemporary psychoanalysts still insisted on calling their theories psychoanalytical. They treat psychoanalysis as a generic term. Freud characterized psychoanalysis as the name of (1) a procedure for the investigation of mental processes which are almost inaccessible in any other way, (2) of a method (based upon that investigation) for the treatment of neurotic disorders, and (3) of a collection of psychological information obtained along those lines, which is gradually being accumulated into a new scientific discipline (Freud 1923a). Although this characterization of psychoanalysis is an operative definition and not a definition of substance, it obliges the contemporary theories to at least abide by the three parameters in Freud's operational definition if they want to claim any relation to psychoanalysis. Usurping the term reveals the inadequacies of the contemporary schools, because if one of them wants to call itself psychoanalysis it has to show that it has the equivalent of Freud's three characterizations of psychoanalysis, i.e., a specific procedure of investigating what claims to be its subject-matter, and that procedure is what is used in performing psychotherapy and a scientific or even a simple theoretical formulation of the data it collects. This is not a hegemonic statement based on a Freudian claim of a trademark of ownership of the term psychoanalysis. It is a statement justified and supported by two arguments: (1) Freudian *Psychoanalysis* is still the only theory that was able to outlive its distortion and the constant attack on its original components. Psychoanalysis constitutes—by now—the background of the Western culture's conception of the psychical aspects of the individual, including what those schools of thought claim to have added. It is the main thread in the fabric of the human societies everywhere there is a society. The Western culture is the culture of the subject (Laplanche 1989) and his psychical attribute in particular. (2) Like very few other theories in the history of epistemology that were indispensable and imperative in the birth and the evolution of other branches of knowledge (sciences) psychoanalysis proved to be more than just an informative theory of the individual. There are new theories that would have been impossible to exist the way they are now without the influence of psychoanalytic thinking. The structural approach to anthropology, sociology, and child psychology is the outcome of psychoanalytic investigation of the structure of the psyche instead of its functional qualities. The two features mentioned are attributes that pertain distinctly to the classical theory, and existed in varied forms throughout the course of its development. Even in the hypnosis phase, hypnosis was a procedure to investigate and to be used as therapy. It was the means to finding and postulating a theory of catharsis. Those postulates were the first breakthrough toward assimilating the new discoveries in the social fabric of the society. Psychoanalysis changed traditional social and moral conceptions, while the contemporary theories have attempted to change psychoanalysis. No contemporary school could claim that it has influenced anything outside the field of psychopathology and psychotherapy, or that it proved to have given rise to any other theory in the field of the humanities. Furthermore, a few informative theories—like the theory of gravity—gave definitive information that generated a new conception of what they formulated in their final format. It generated the notions that were basic in the theory of relativity. Therefore, those particular theories, which psychoanalysis belongs to, outlive the information they provide and lead to other horizons of information.

For now we could say that what we examined about the evolution of the theory of psychoanalysis was its informative quality. Freud was torn between his ambition to formulate a new and comprehensive informative theory of the human psyche, but intuitively realized that what he and his disciples were stepping toward was much bigger and important. He did not have in mind the distinction between an *informative* and a *structural* theory, but he was gifted enough to realize that he did not come up with that final informative theory about the psyche, and maybe he never would. The problem, as many signs indicate now, was his struggles with the subject matter of his search: what was psychoanalysis about? What firm information did it provide about the psyche? Would it be enough to claim the birth of a scientific discipline? During almost half a century of researching and theorizing, some of Freud's main works were attempts to consolidate his contributions in order to offer the new and ever-widening field of the humanities a structuralized modality of the human psyche based on what he considered informative material. His attempts were unproductive. The early theory of catharsis and the role of sexuality in it gave way to the theory of the dynamics of symptom formation and defenses. This in turn gave way to the structural point of view in ego psychology. Those attempts produced uninspiring informative formulations. The attempts at foreclosing the theory prematurely did not sit well with Freud when his disciples tried (Adler, Jung, Stekle, Rank, and Ferenczi). Even when he attempted that—as is the case with ego psychology—he revisited the concept of anxiety (Freud 1926d) and shed doubt about its conclusiveness as a statement about the psyche, thus undoing the theory of the ego. Yet, contrary to many critiques of Freud's three metapsychologies, metapsychology saved psychoanalysis from losing its bearings as a structural theory and made it, in a peculiar way, the most influential theory in Western culture and modern civilization of the twentieth century. He tried and failed to foreclose the theory several time, although he denied his disciples that privilege. But as we will see later, Freud's leadership of the psychoanalytic movement was most valued in his constant resistance to proclaim a final informative theory of psychoanalysis. What he left us is several significant attempts at configuring one, but did not claim any of those attempts to contain the elements of a structural theory of psychoanalysis. Despite the disparate efforts made by his disciples—after his passing—they failed to find one definitive final informative theory to hang on to. Most of the efforts were to choose the most likely aspect of the human psyche to make it the central core of the theory and do their best to find a place for the relegated concepts. Anything that looked like the most prevailing notion or a last formulation by Freud was inflated to look like *the* informative theory of the psyche. By the 1970s, psychoanalysis was heading to what became in the 1990s a real crisis. The crises caused hasty and improvised searches for a replacement for a final informative theory of psychoanalysis that did not exist in the first place. Although psychoanalysis is still the most important theory of modern times which has given birth to Western culture, it is not yet with a final informative theory.[1]

This raises a multifaceted question: Are there any connections between the past, the present, and the future of psychoanalysis? The concerns about the future of psychoanalysis were usually related to its theory, but proved to be more complex, as mentioned before. Psychoanalysis was fated to be a complex combination of theoretical issues and professional matters, with serious personal oddities. It started in the field of treatment and psychotherapy but it immediately became a theoretical endeavor, due to Freud's very spontaneous insights in the psychodynamics of the hysterical condition. Unintentionally, Freud had the insight that every progress in understanding a symptom in a hysterical patient improves the understanding of the hysterical patient and not only the process of symptom formation. This was an insight in the link between investigation and treatment and between treatment and theory (Holzman and Aronson 1992). It resulted in finding better ways of treatment than hypnosis, which happened a few years later when he resorted to free association instead. The beginning of psychoanalysis entwined theory and practice in a way that remained an intrinsic attribute in any possible evaluation of its condition at any point in its history. No wonder that analysts were always unsettled about *which the cart is and which the horse was*! However, those issues that look to us now as matter of fact were subject to disagreements and the idiosyncrasies of the individual followers of Freud. The most peculiar thing about that complex set-up was the form it took in the history of the movement. The future of psychoanalysis has always been a concern from the early beginnings as the movement was searching for an identity. The general trend was to identify psychoanalysis as a profession of psychotherapy. However, the problems of the profession were disguised by changing them to problems pertaining to the designated function of the psychoanalytic institution (IPA). This way, the confusion about psychoanalysis as an informative theory or a structural theory, a movement or a school of thought, a profession or a discipline, got worse because not all those issues pertain to the organization of psychoanalysis. Nevertheless, the organization assumed the responsibility for making those differentiations. Another problem was added to the difficulty of discerning the issue of the theory from the issue of the profession. The institutional matters relating to those two issues were wrapped in some sort of secrecy (as will be shown a little later) and the membership was excluded from both knowing them or solving them. This peculiar state of affairs created an atmosphere of tension within the institution, which developed to become in its own right a threat to its future. The most evident leftover traces of that tension are manifested now in unusual concerns about the functioning of the institutions of psychoanalysis, nationally and internationally, irrespective of the subject. I would even intimate that the present crisis in psychoanalysis (see Edelson 1988; Fayek 2014) is just the continuation or the most recent version of the crisis of psychoanalysis between 1911–1913. What happened then was an anxiety about the future of the theory, the profession, and the role of the institution. Presently, whenever there are concerns about psychoanalysis and its future we notice the same feature: all three issues amalgamate in one big anxiety. To be more specific, I would run a quick and general review of the anxiety about the future (fate!) of psychoanalysis. Freud and the early pioneers worried about the outward rejection of the public and the medical community of the early findings and formulations of psychoanalysis. Crossing that bridge led to worries about the disciples deviating from the core of the doctrine. Those concerns about adhering to the core premises of the theory were unjustified, because the theory was not in a stable or final state at any time during Freud's life. He and his disciples were unable, at any time, to come up with a final configuration of the psyche, or a stable conception of what was to be the future arena of research. Therefore, Freud's concerns were basically about loyalty to him; a concern that made Ferenczi and Jones suggest forming a secret committee in 1912 to protect Freud from the attacks he was exposed to from some disciples.[2] There was, however, some foundation for those early apprehensions, because it was not long after two main contributors to the evolution of the theory (Adler and Jung) showed the aspiration to separate from the movement and form their own theories and movements. Therefore, we should restate the concerns of the early years of the movement—concerns about loyalty to Freud masked by worries about the theory and its purity, the profession, and the stability of the institution, all in one intertwined worry.

The core of the doctrine during Freud's lifetime was changing according to what he considered the main issue of the psyche: sex, repression, the unconscious, defense, metapsychology, topography, structural conception of the psyche, etc. His concerns must have been about something else than the integrity of his doctrine. He was—matter of fact—the most prolific of the membership and the source of most of the novelties in the theory, therefore it was the custom to wait for his ideas before anyone would suggest something unrelated. Moreover, he was the approving authority and the one to canonize any of the pioneer's additions to the theory. The theory was advancing well toward its future, yet the inveterate concern about the future of psychoanalysis remained active. It was disguised in terms of questioning the loyalty and adherence to the "Freudian Movement," more than to him or his theory. From the beginning there was fusion between Freud and psychoanalysis and devotion to one was also commitment to the other. Although this is something we would frown upon nowadays it was—in actuality and practically—what sustained psychoanalysis and protected it from possible disintegration during many and long years of uncertainty. Better, what we would regard as critical now, regarding the link made between Freud and psychoanalysis, was what made psychoanalysis endure the early attacks as a revolutionary conception of the human subject. It attracted many gifted people in this way. The problem with that is not what it was then but how the implicit devotion to Freud's authority bequeathed to the psychoanalytic institution still lingers in the background of the present problems of psychoanalysis. Freud gave the institution its authority but after his death the relationship between the institution and psychoanalytic authority did not change.

After Freud's death, the link between the authority of the institution and psychoanalysis should have changed, but it perniciously became a prototype that resisted change. The loyalty to Freud had its justification and served a very important function. But, when it was transferred onto the International Psychoanalytic Association some individual analysts were openly vying for control of the institution, because dominating the institution would make them embody its authority. Due to certain circumstances—that will be mentioned later—the early analysts who took charge of the institution assumed the function of masters of the profession. This transformation sustained the concerns about the future of psychoanalysis and maintained the internal tension within the institution. The IPA assumed the function of the "Guardian of the Classical Theory," and the elected presidents and their assisting committees "supposedly" somehow, incarnated Freud's authority. Since establishing the IPA in 1910, there was a tacit understanding that certain members would be occupying—on rotating basis—the president's seat and the other positions on the executive committees. Continuing this tacit tradition after Freud's death created an inner circle of members, who either claimed or supported some theoretical trends which made them the accepted extensions of the Freudian doctrine. The members of that inner circle had quasi-dominance on the theoretical future of psychoanalysis. They exercised control over the politics of the IPA regarding training, publishing, and, to some degree, supervision of the local societies and institutes. Theoretical dominance came in a natural way with the closeness to the centers of authority in the IPA, and group transference on those governing figures played a major role. The expansion and increase in membership everywhere created personal competitions between the big figures in the institution. This feature still plagues all the local societies, as it existed from the time that the secret committee was established. Freud's presence kept those competitive urges under wraps and control. Those tensions did not spare most of psychoanalytic institutions everywhere. Starting in England in the late 1940s, Klein and Anna Freud had their spats (King and Steiner 1991). The British Society opted to contain the split by recognizing two groups representing the two camps. Then a middle group formed a third camp. In the 1950s in France, there were the two major splits that opened the floodgates to endless splits. After Lacan and Lagache declared differences with Nacht, who was the analyst most close to the IPA, they lost their membership in the institution. However, Lagache and his followers with the exception of Lacan and his group were later reinstated and formed a new society recognized by the IPA. Lacan formed an independent group and called it the "Freudian School." It took some time for Lacan's school to breed a litany of subgroups and the psychoanalytic scene in France became quite active, productive and much more expressive of the spirit of French culture. In the United States there was an apparent stability under the domination of ego-psychology and the leadership of Hartmann. However, after his passing, a few things happened in sequence that resulted in chaos and disintegration. Ego-psychologists, having been freed from Hartmann's influence, were able to discuss the weaknesses in that theory, thus dethroning the ideal theory. This trend encouraged the introduction of Kleinians' theoretical formulations which was an anathema before. The lack of a unified theoretical base for analysis (as it was in Hartmann's time) was exasperated by opening training to non-medical candidates, which introduces new liberal ways of thinking both in terms of theory and practice.

The aforementioned lack of solid knowledge of basic Freud in the fourth generation of trainees led to the free-for-all forming schools of psychoanalysis with no means to evaluate them. In South America—as far as I know—psychoanalysis was equally diversified into schools and trends. Loyalty to the IPA failed to maintain order and it had to give in and accept the status quo. The IPA did not object to that and tolerated this unusual arrangement. It even condoned it (Wallerstein 1988; 1990). Wallerstein (2005) admitted that accepting theoretical polarity of psychoanalysis was politically expedient at the time to avoid the disintegration of the IPA. Some of the contemporary schools were ready to desert the IPA and form their own associations. However, the deterioration in of psychoanalysis, irrespective of which school suffered more of that deterioration, obligates all the psychoanalytic institutions—national and international—to deal with the problem. They have been doing that all over the world with no promising results. The situation does not bode well for the future of psychoanalysis, that is, if there is a future for psychoanalysis. The obvious reason is that both theoretical issues and practice matters are badly affected by the chaotic state of psychoanalysis in all those different places. The fusion of theory and practice is in much worse condition than at any time in the history of psychoanalysis. At the moment, the fusion is not only a fact in reality but has also become confusion in the minds of the psychoanalysts. Psychoanalysts of this generation are not facing up to the theoretical condition of psychoanalysis because they are not competent and knowledgeable enough to do that. Therefore most of the effort—at least in the United States—is spent in trying to improve the institution hoping that this will improve training and practice. They are not willing or able to identify the difficulties in each area separately to approach it with the proper method. This confusion is paramount but with very superficial differences between the regional institutions. Furthermore, any attempt at isolating an issue in this confused state of mind to tackle it better, for instance, arguing the issue of whether analysis is a psychology of the intrapsychical or the interpersonal is avoided vehemently, or engrossed in personal and subjective nature. The fusion of the theory and professional practice does not facilitate making the more fundamental distinction between psychoanalysis as an informative theory and a structural theory (has core premises to disclose). It is necessary to examine the present situation within the psychoanalytic circle first to assess the claim that psychoanalysts are trying to give their discipline (profession) a future. If there is a possibility for turning around its present—rather desperate—state and finding a way to save it in the future we should consider it carefully; there are several claims to that effect in the last forty years to no avail. They all take the direction of improving the informative theory of psychoanalysis or replacing it with another one, while the objective is to move from the informative theory to the structural theory of analysis. There were few fleeting attempts at making structural improvements to the theory (Bion 1963; Gill 1979; 1982; Green 1999; 2005; Kohut 1987; Lacan 1977a; 1977b; Laplanche 1989; Matte-Blanco 1975; Schafer 1976; Stolorow 2002). However those attempts were either too brilliant to be adopted by main stream analysts, were heavily loaded with personal narcissistic interests, or were simply of no value. Nevertheless, there is less work done on the core propositions of the structural theory of psychoanalysis and there is a serious need to link psychoanalysis with other idiographic sources of knowledge to create a psychoanalysis that is part of a culture.

The daunting disagreements in the history of psychoanalysis seem to be about a theory that is never wrong but at the same time permanently unsatisfactory. The analytic theory as an informative theory was never fully satisfactory and still is not. It comprises vague and unclear concepts, partial and impartial points of view, hastily formed conclusions and sometimes advocates definitive ideas that proven wrong. A good example of those attempts is the call in the 1970s to work toward a clinical theory that should be the only informative theory of psychoanalysis, and give up the rest of the analytic theory (Holt 1976; G. Klein 1976). Notwithstanding all those causes and excuses, the need for an analytic theory imposes itself on us. The identity of the psychoanalyst as a member of a professional institution which is also a scientific association is a complicating issue and should not impose on any effort to think about future psychoanalysis. The question that stems from these arguments is simple: Is there a future for psychoanalysis that will come from a new, improved comprehensive informative theory, or should a structural theory of psychoanalysis be identified, defined, and enhanced to become the basis of future psychoanalysis? There is another related question: Is future psychoanalysis that is based on structural theory going to be a clinical discipline or something else?

NOTES

1. Copernicus's heliocentric model of the universe and Darwin's theory of evolution are the two other theories that shaped the mentality of Western thinkers.

2. Freud's concerns about loyalty to him and the psychoanalytic movement is cogently expressed: "It would be sad if one could find oneself deceived after living together for fifteen or seventeen years. . . . I have become an invalid with diminished powers of working and in enfeebled frame of mind which turns away from any increased burden and no longer feel equal to any caring care. I survived the committee that was to have been my successor. Perhaps I shall survive the International Association. It is hoped that psychoanalysis will survive me. But it all gives a somber end to one's life" (Jones 1957, Vol. III, pp. 68–69).

ONE

The Informative Theory of Psychoanalysis

A few weeks after my first complete reading of *The Freudian* text, a very nagging question formed in spite of my admiration of it: What have I learned of the theory it was about? There was no conclusive answer: so much and yet almost nothing.[1] A little after, I wondered about evaluating the work since there was no other theory of the psyche to compare with. Psychoanalysis was criticized by many (Eysenck 1963; Popper 1974) but was still uncontested by any other serious replacement theories.

I found an answer to the first question after a second reading when I gradually made a distinction between psychoanalysis as a theory of information about the psyche, i.e., an informative theory, and as a method of thinking about it, which makes it a structural theory too. Most theories are either functional or structural because what decides the nature of the theory are both its subject matter and the method of studying that subject matter. Theories in physical sciences are functional because their subject matter is measurable, invariable and constant, thus they could be observed more or less in isolation of the impact of other factors on it. It is easier to think of a physical phenomenon in terms of cause-effect relations, due to the fact that the scientist can exclude by elimination the factors that do not play a causative role in their formation. In other terms, physical sciences theories are built of *deductive* observations of causal relationships that explain the subject matter. Theories in human sciences are differently formulated. The subject matter of a human science is intrinsically interconnected with other human phenomena. As such, the best the human scientist would aspire to is to use *inductive* thinking to reconstruct the specific events that led to the human condition he is studying. Therefore, theories in human sciences are not functional, because they do not seek a functional link between causes and effects. They are structural because they study the underlying human structure that produced the phenomenon they study. The Freudian doctrine comprises those two kinds of theories and could sustain both deductive and inductive thinking. Psychoanalysis—in one way—is an informative theory; a theory that has concluding statements about a set of individual issues like dreams, symptom formation, repression of certain urges and thought, etc. It also has a theory of the dynamic interrelationship between the pressure of the endosomatic stimulus on the mind generating mental representations, the impact of the stage of development on the pressure put on the mind at that stage, and the possible normal and pathological outcome of that tripartite configuration.

The second question was practically answered during the course of studying and practicing psychoanalysis and reading the literature that eventually became the literature of current psychoanalysis. I realized that Freud disagreed with Adler's *Individual Psychology,* Jung's *Analytic Psychology,* Stekle's *Off Handed and Unsubstantiated Ideas,* and Rank's *Birth Trauma* for the same reason: foreclosing on the subject prematurely. He would have disagreed with the modifications introduced to his theory over the years, and with the new suggested replacement theories. He consistently refused turning a description of a process into fixed information. I realized that Freud knew by intuition that his theory was not a theory of functions or of informative nature, but a theory of the structures of the phenomena that it dealt and deals with. He refused to build psychoanalysis on foreclosed ideas or mechanisms—like Rank's birth trauma, or the place of a child in the family (Adler)—and making them explanatory "Modus Oparandi" or causations of the psychical life of the individual.

Despite what seemed like looking for such final explanation or explanations—in some of his renowned works—he was always turning the explanation into a *problematic* that demanded explanations. Freud's theory of the psyche—in my view—was a project in progress. It was not totally adequate at any stage of its evolution and development, but it was uniquely distinct. Every stage of its evolution was improving the "information" and the causal explanation it was offering, but was also leading to an unidentified end. The end of the sexual aetiology of the psychoneuroses led to discovering the concept of *Trieb* and infantile sexuality. Yet, that advancement was uncovering the limitations of the concept of the libido and prepared for the paper on "narcissism." In better words, the difference between the Freudian doctrine and any other theory of the psyche is that it always turned a functional conception into structural make-up and pushed toward more than its functionality provided. Psychoanalysis was a project in progress to discovering the structural basis of the human subject and not his dreams, melancholy, or sexual preferences, etc. My admiration of the Freudian doctrine did not cease all those years when I was searching for answers to the two questions. The reason was and still is that psychoanalysis is not an informative theory of the psyche; it is a structural theory of the human subject. Two more readings of the full text, one of which was with a group of human scientists and thinkers that took four years to finish,[2] allowed me to read Freud with both sides of the theory next to each other. I first realized that Freud discovered very early that psychoanalysis is a method of thinking and not a theory of thoughts (information). When I first made the comparisons between his way of thinking and the others who were about him when he was exploring this dark part of the human mind, and even those who came after him, it became clear that psychoanalysis has two histories: an *explicit* history of discoveries that look like final reconstruction of the psyche, and an *implicit* core that kept it growing and expanding and having such an impact and influence on the Western culture as a whole. An example of the dual theoretical background of psychoanalysis is clear in the culture's acceptance of the place of sexuality in daily life (psychoanalytic information), and the social assimilating of the notion that the link between cause and effect in human behaviors is not direct but is a complex process of transformations (structurally different from common thinking of causations). The distinction between the informative and the structural nature of the psychoanalytical theory makes it possible to understand the rancor in the psychoanalytic institution. The pleas for replacing the classical theory, or making major modification to it, is about issues in the informative aspect of the theory. Yet, the structural theory—the core of psychoanalysis—is not just overlooked; it is not yet properly identified or defined to be addressed. To get to the structural aspect of the theory of psychoanalysis we have to review the informative theory(ies) with an eye on two things: Freud's ingenious inductive work to elicit the core attribute of every particular discovery he made, and the inevitability of reaching the point when he had to move from the detailed discoveries to the core propositions of the theory, which kept it from imploding.

FREUD AND PSYCHOANALYSIS: A SYNONYMY

The place Freud occupies in psychoanalysis is unique compared with the place other pioneers, great thinkers, and theoreticians had in their fields.[3] Those great people were admired, respected, and always received proper esteem from their successors. Freud had some of those niceties, but they were always just part of idealizing the man. Seldom do we find a theorist who was idealized by his disciples (except maybe Einstein), but Freud's special place in psychoanalysis is heavily colored by idealization, naturally creating its antithesis at a certain level of awareness. Idealizing Freud is not something to sneer at or disparage, because it came from the same people who learned from him about it and knew well the neurotic base of such relationship. He revealed the psychological principal of idealization to his followers, and those followers who were supposed to free people from that bind were on the contrary entangled in it, sometimes to a funny extent. Yet, Freud expected idealization and did not discourage it, and analysts liked idealizing him. This idealization created a difficult overlap between the man and his doctrine, which contributed to the crisis of psychoanalysis of late, as I will discuss in chapter 2.

I mentioned that feature in Freud's biography to elucidate three aspects that have a significant impact on the present status of psychoanalysis and on its future: (1) Theories are isolated thought entities that provide specific information and are "one shot" insights that lead to other theories, which usually surpass them. Their authors typically work more on creating other theories, or on theories of others. Psychoanalysis was different in that aspect. Freud remained—for over fifty years—the most creative and authoritative author who went beyond his own theory and advanced and developed it better than all his disciples (maybe with some exceptions from Abraham). Hence, he maintained a distinct position in the movement of psychoanalysis. His dominant place in the history of psychoanalysis is justified, yet his idealization, inevitable as it was, became a problem after his passing. (2) Freud presented the first breakthrough in recognizing and describing the intrapsychical dynamics of the individual, although he did not have solid clinical proof for his conceptions. However, he stood firm on the issue that humans are psychological beings who could be analyzed and understood; they are beings that their life could not be explained by external forces alone. It seems from the way that his discoveries were received that they were convincing enough without the need for solid clinical evidence. He had the stature and the convincing prowess to save the psychoanalytic movement from early dismissal merely by the style of his writings, which was evidently very novel at the time. He kept the external attacks on psychoanalysis at bay by continuous innovative and groundbreaking writings, and dealing with the internal disputes between the disciples, preventing them from destroying the analytic movement. (3) Freud's prolific abilities and gift in presenting his views to a hostile world—either gaining its support or forcing its respect—was a mixture of solid knowledge of what he was advocating and a talent for convincing both his followers and his adversaries. His followers were always a step behind him in developing their ideas and contribution to the theory. *This is a situation that would easily create jealousy, and turn it into idealization.* His world stature and talent in gathering support from the best and well-known thinkers of his time was also a blessing that his followers benefited from. Despite everything negative that could be said about Freud's stature in psychoanalysis, the shortcomings of the classical theory as we see it now, and the clambering to replace it or to occupy his place in the psychoanalytic movement, it is impossible to deny that he is one of the most impressive thinkers of modern history. Even with the declining stature of psychoanalysis his name is still at the center of any human controversy, whether seriously considered or sarcastically mentioned.

The three aspects of being an imposing person and the sole creator of psychoanalysis, his importance in giving the psychoanalytic theory its foundational credibility, and making psychoanalysis a lasting issue in our culture are basic issues in arguing the future of psychoanalysis, especially that the name Freud has become synonymous with the term psychoanalysis. Therefore, Freud's emergence from Vienna's medical circle to create the psychoanalytic cause and its scene says many things about the emergence of psychoanalysis from the limitations of mid-nineteenth century medicine.

There are no beginnings in history but only interesting starting points. By the end of the eighteenth century, Pinel liberated the residences of the Salpetriere hospital and called them patients, i.e., people who deserve medical treatment. In fact, by calling people with mental disorders patients he freed the medical profession from being excluded from the treatment of a population of patients that were seen as belonging to mysticism and not medicine. He began a true revolution in the concept of the human subject. Some important pioneers followed suit in France and central Europe. In the decades that followed, great strides were taken in identifying mental disorders and defining them. It is enough to mention Kraepelin to remind people of the great pioneers of the eighteenth century and the first half of the nineteenth century who created psychiatry as a specialty in medicine and prepared the grounds for the second half of the revolution. They even worked on systems to classify mental disorders and established early nosological entities that identify the kind of mental functions, which are affected in each entity. They were able in this way to identify the neuroses, which were considered psychological disorders, and strictly speaking, not mental disorders. They liberated the human subject from religious mythology and from the strait jacket of bio-physiological existence.

By the end of the nineteenth century Europe was buzzing with physicians coming up with new ideas and new methods of explorations, challenging the establishment of medicine in regard to mental disorders, and most of all accepting the involvement of the emotional factors in the clinical pictures. Hypnosis became an intriguing issue in Europe when Mesmer suggested a different type of energy that could be manipulated to release the patient from certain psychological conditions. He used hypnosis as a therapeutic means and gave it a quasi-medical nature. On the Germanic side of Europe, most of the endeavors were toward improving the conditions that allow evolution to take care of progress in medicine. In England the effort was not to deny the new advancements in the field of mental diseases, but to refer them to known neuro-physio-psychological sources.

However, the big buzz came from France. In Nancy both Bernheim and Liebeault used hypnosis with patients and discovered a great deal about the involvement of life experiences in creating symptoms, especially in hysteria. They even used verbal suggestion—a non-medical process—as therapy. Something similar happened in Paris where Charcot and Janet built their theories of the neurotic conditions (hypotheses) on what hypnosis revealed to them about the undeclared emotional life of the patient. This shift was possible only to physicians because they were the professionals who had the right to treat patients. However, we should mention that Freud showed in many ways that he was not interested in medicine as a profession (general practice) and was inclined from very early on to leave it if he had the chance. Freud was, thus, one of the dozens of physicians who were exploring, theorizing, and creating within medicine a new profession.

That chance to leave medicine came to Freud when Breuer introduced him to hypnotic work with hysterical patients in the late nineteenth century. Although dozens of keen and interested physicians were actively trying new ideas and ways, and experimenting with new approaches in their fields, Freud's emergence among them was different and unintentionally unique. Instead of just following what Breuer was doing Freud went directly to the heart of the matter: a theory of psychopathology. He was eager to learn from Liebeault in Paris then from Bernheim in Nancy. His experience with them formed two budding ideas: (1) there must be a way other than hypnosis to discover the causation of hysteria, and (2) it is not what is repressed that causes the psychoneuroses. These two preoccupations convincingly demonstrate his contribution in the *Studies on Hysteria* (1895d), particularly in the case of Katharina. He was able to reconstruct the young woman's unconscious causation of her symptoms only from her conscious recall of certain events and passing thoughts.

Freud separated from Breuer after Breuer's reaction to Anna O.'s transference-love. Contrary to Breuer's reaction to the complication of transference, Freud showed interest in the phenomenon itself. He did not panic when he realized that it is one of the outcomes of the intimate relationship with patients that hypnosis creates, especially female patients. He realized that there was more to discover, and most of all he seemed to realize that there is more in that discovery than the mere treatment of patients. Pointing out and comparing Freud's contribution to Breuer's work in book they shared writing is not idealizing Freud in disguise. The case of Katharina, in his shared book with Breuer (1895d), demonstrates an early inclination to "read the symptom" not just explore the repressed. He became interested in the process of repression more than the repressed; consequently he abandoned hypnosis a few years later. Then, came a stroke of genius: he realized that he has to understand normal psychical life if he is to understand it's pathological forms. In a letter to Fliess (May 25, 1895) he said: "Actually, a satisfactory general conception of neuropsychotic disturbances is impossible if one cannot link it with clear assumptions about normal mental processes."

There is something extraordinary in that insight. Freud spent the five years after publishing the book on hysteria with Breuer writing snippets about insignificant issues with the exception of the two papers on the neuropsychosis of defense (Freud 1894a; 1896b). Those two papers were—in fact—extracts from his *Project for a Scientific Psychology* (1950a), which we learned about after his passing. Therefore, it is reasonable assume that Freud spent those five years between the book on hysteria and *The Interpretation of Dreams* (1900a) occupied by works of purely psychological nature. After the book on dreams Freud spent four years working and writing about "the normal" and even banal phenomenons, considering that he was a neurophysiologist and a practicing physician. *The Interpretation of Dreams* (1900a), *The Psychopathology of Everyday Life* (1901b), and *Jokes and Their Relations to the Unconscious* (1905c) were statements of fact that Freud had moved to psychology and left medicine behind, and psychoanalysis was by then severed from both the academic psychologies of Wundt (and maybe Brentano, too!) and from medicine. If we compare Freud with the other pioneers at his time we cannot miss the difference: every step he made was a step in a long walk, while all others—like Adler and Stekle—took a few steps and considered them the end of their journeys. *Freud was not yet inclined to create a theory of the psyche; he was simply exploring what he might have thought then to be the material for an informative theory of the psyche.*

He emerged among very active and creative physicians but was a different kind of a pioneer. He was a man on the trail of something unclear or defined that was beckoning him from the future, and not a man with just the ambition to make a discovery and enjoy the status it would give him. He worked alone for over a decade discovering matters that were unwelcomed by mainstream medical professionals. He persisted and did not waver, clearly because he realized that each discovery was incomplete and only a step before another more significant in the offing. After a while he attracted the attention of men like him who were also liberated from the strict medical model and wanted to learn about the psychological aspects of the human mind. They came from around Vienna and from other parts of the continent. It is important to say, that they were as gifted and motivated, but some were looking prematurely for the end of the journey. To clarify this point, I mention Adler and Jung. They had gifted minds and possibly even more gifted than the rest (Jung was convincingly a bright person). Compared with Freud, Freud was not definite yet about what he was looking for, while those two were hasty in their satisfaction with what they had achieved, and thought that there was nothing more worthy of waiting for. Thus, they parted company. Jones called it defection when it was just them finding a path of their own to follow. Nevertheless, when we compare psychoanalysis with *individual psychology* or *analytic psychology* it becomes clear that Freud was different. The influence psychoanalysis had on psychiatry and psychology is impressive enough to point out the difference. Freud was not after innovating something but after something novel.

This initial phase in the history of psychoanalysis could be described as a phase of growing interest, in different parts of the world, in the new Freudian conception of the "psychological"; a new and intriguing aspect of the human subject. The events of the next ten years of the life of the movement were dominated by the curiosity of a few individuals who went to Freud to gain insights in something very new. Freud and those colleagues were interested discovering the working of repression and searching for the main originator of the psychoneuroses. They were amazed by their discoveries. They spent those years comparing notes about the consistency of their discoveries with Freud's main work. However, when the novelty waned gradually, the *content* of what was discovered took center stage. A few lost their curiosity about the processes that create the psychological phenomena and concentrated on developing the content of their discoveries. Better, when psychoanalysis was a process of discovering and not a theory about what is discovered, things were going smoothly between Freud and the analysts around him. But when they came to the point of comparing what is discovered, disagreement about what was right and was "less right" erupted. The few who lost interest in studying the process left after a while, thinking that they had gained what they came to learn, and had the notion that they could have their own schools. Their discoveries were accumulating but without any central theoretical core that would bind them in that theory.

Just after the book on jokes Freud published *Three Essays on the Theory of Sexuality* (1905d). This last work in particular revealed that he was shifting his attention from the almost mechanistic theory of catharsis—a theory of repression as a *function* of the sexual urges and their associated moral values—to the *structure* of the repressed.[4] The book on sexuality was the subtle announcement of a change in the informative theory of psychoanalysis, because it introduced three new concepts to the informative theory: (1) the concept of *Trieb* as the instigator of the psychological manifestation of a physical urge and the effect of a physical pressure of an urge like sex on the mind to react, and of the concept of libido as the sexual energy that has a direct relationship to anxiety changed to be more the energy of the *Trieb* that has qualitative attributes as well. (2) *Trieb* as a bipolar entity in the sense that its activation activates its antithesis at the same time (sexual and self-preservation), thus the psychical representation of the *Trieb* is considered a complex structure that is amenable to analysis. (3) Sexuality as one end of a *Triebhaft* bipolarity is a complex entity in its own right. Its complexity comes from its multiple resources in different erotogenic zones in the body. It starts fragmented in childhood and gets integrated in the process of maturation to become what is known in adulthood as sex.

Historically speaking, the conflicts Freud had with dissenting colleagues looks like personal conflicts or disagreements about his theoretical stand. But when we look closely at introducing infantile sexuality to the explanation of the sexual aetiology of psychoneuroses a different picture arises. The dissenters were convinced that the aetiology they are suggesting is better than sexuality, which Freud was proposing. Freud was not fully satisfied with his own proposed aetiology because it was used as a set urge when infantile sexuality showed that it has several forms. He found out that the problem with sexuality is the nature of the "sexual" as a *Trieb*. Sexuality as a physical urge does not explain all its manifestation as a *Trieb*. Its pressure on the mind to act (1905d, 20) is much more complex to just be considered an urge with predictable social concomitants. The dissention was about a theory of psychoanalysis that is evolving from the concrete and static toward a theory of transformation[5] and dynamics. Better, Freud did not approve the propositions suggested by his adversaries because they deemed psychoanalysis a theory of information when he had the insight that whatever is discovered was just preliminary to further discoveries and should not be treated as information.

Medicine is founded on solid information that could be changed but not totally annulled. Thus, what was marginally accepted in the medical circles is that sexuality could instigate repression, i.e., cause it. Infantile sexuality changed the theory of symptom formation from an appendage to the medical conception of pathology and treatment to a branch of knowledge with its independent theory, and in all likelihood an independent profession. After the *Three Essays* and until Freud's papers on technique, he published few works on the application of psychoanalysis in different fields of knowledge, and the two cases of Hans (1909b) and the Rat Man (1909d). Yet, he published only two significant papers on clinical matters: *Character and Anal Erotism* (1908b) and *Family Romance* (1909c). The two papers were very different in dealing with the clinical issues they raised: character formation and childhood fantasy and their link with the Oedipus complex. They contained psychoanalytic information about clinical matters in a style of writing that medical people neither welcomed nor understood. They were also foreign to some followers of Freud who did not feel good about unfolding the topics they considered fixed (the Oedipus complex) or sexuality and the libido. Adler and Stekle left in 1911, followed by Jung's resignation from the International Psychoanalytic Association, which required a major reconstruction of the psychoanalytic movement including refining the theoretical mix. By 1910, psychoanalysis was about ready for a new change in the informative theory, which was taking shape and direction.

The volatility and the way Adler, Jung, and Stekle dissented affected the main stream of the psychoanalytic movement. Freud worried about the future of psychoanalysis. Some of his most loyal disciples expressed some concerns too. Ferenczi suggested to Ernest Jones to form a committee of few of the devotees to Freud and the strong advocates of psychoanalysis in Europe, to secure a disciplined advocacy and to maintain the core proposals of psychoanalysis. He envisaged that this committee could avoid in the future something similar to what happened with the dissenters. The physical impracticality of the idea (forming a committee that cannot easily be called upon for meetings) made Jones suggest a committee of undeclared members who knew each other secretly and could thus communicate freely in spite of their scattered places in the world. This secret committee is known in the history of psychoanalysis as "The Committee." It was formed by six of Freud's closest disciples and him making it a committee of seven. They tried not to accept in the psychoanalytic movement anyone who did not vouch for the concepts of repression, the unconscious, infantile sexuality, defense, etc. This committee was to be limited to the members whom Freud approved and would function secretly as the guardian of the purity of the theory. The members would provide the support Freud's needed in the International Association with their secretive status and their theoretical dominance in the psychoanalytic community. We have to note that the members of the secrete committee offered themselves as possible targets and defenders of any criticism directed at Freud or the theory.

Freud's reaction to the formation of the committee is telling. After the first meeting of the committee in 1913, Freud talked about not worrying anymore about the future of psychoanalysis. He said that the existence of this committee would make living and dying easier. He was convinced that he did not finish what he was doing yet and might not be able to manage doing that either. He said that the committee has taken off of him the burden of minding the future of psychoanalysis, and that he "can calmly follow his path to the end." His reaction reveals his sense of destiny and vocation, and his fear and worry that psychoanalysis might vanish after his death. He also felt that what he would leave behind could die if not continued and preserved by analysts who were willing to protect it from distortion and defend it when criticized. In few words: Freud's reaction to the formation of the committee revealed his sense of importance to psychoanalysis (maybe to history itself), and a sense of devotion to the psychoanalytic movement. It also conveyed a sense of relief and freedom to embark on some major revisions of his theory, which took place between 1911 and 1917.

A new phase in the history of the informative theory of psychoanalysis began about 1911. After several works on the application of psychoanalysis in other areas of the humanities, Freud got to the long awaited papers on technique; how to practice the informative aspect of psychoanalysis.[6] The papers on technique constituted *a protocol* for the practice. They later became the benchmark for the practice of psychoanalysis proper in contrast with the rest of the psychotherapies which started to sprout around, which had to have their own protocols to justify their existence. His main and basic recommendations for a proper practice of psychoanalysis (then and still till now) were based purely on the interpretation of free association, and *abstaining* from interfering with the *process* of therapy by mixing any pre-known or external information with the patient's material.[7] He also emphasized the significance of transference and the resolution of its acting-out in analysis as *means* to treatment. The papers were indicative of a change in the direction of revealing the structural nature of the psychoanalytic theory, more than adding something new to the informative aspect of the theory. If the analyst does not use the theory to explain things to the patient and will only interpret the patient's association, then psychoanalysis is a formative process, and not an informative one. Hence, the new emerging theory of psychoanalysis reflected that fundamental change. He concluded his papers on technique with "A Note on the Unconscious" (1912g) ending with it the indelible meaning of the unconscious as a content of rejectionable ideas and urges, and introducing the meaning of the unconscious as a psychical system.

Freud began changing the theory, by 1911, from a theory of discoveries in the provinces of the unconscious to a theory that shapes the mind of the analyst. His writings from the time of the papers on technique were of a leader and a teacher of psychoanalysis. He was showing in most of his works how to discern the Ucs. system from the other two systems: Cs. and the Pcs. (the repressed), thus become a psychoanalyst, not merely someone interested in uncovering the repressed content in some individual phenomena.

FROM THE INFORMATIVE THEORY TO ITS STRUCTURAL BASE

Up until the paper on the "Pleasure Principle" (Freud 1911b) the framework of the catharsis theory was dominating psychoanalysis (and still does to an extent). Originally psychoanalysis endeavored to expose something repressed, and by doing so the effect of the repressed on the patient was supposed to recedes. Although infantile sexuality forced a change to the sexual aetiology of the psychoneuroses, it did not change the notion that what is repressed is still an objectionable sexualized content. The catharsis theory is mainly an informative theory about phenomena of the individual; a theory about psychopathology, dreams, symptom formation, the treatment by psychoanalysis, and about some psychological aspects of some other human phenomena.

The paper on the "Pleasure Principle" introduced to psychoanalysis a new perspective. Freud talked about the manner by which the "wish" starts the process of the formation of the psychical and the duality of pleasure if it was gratified and pain if it was not. He said (almost rephrasing Brentano's idea) that the mind creates a presentation of the object in the mind, judges the presentation, ending with loving or hating it. The newness of this notion is Freud's interest in the *psychology* of the phenomena, which he was discovering and examining as events in the life of the individual. Better, Freud shifted his attention from the psychical phenomena of the individual (like depression) to the individual's creation and formation of those phenomena. For instance, instead of calling sexual perversion fixation on an infantile sexual object, psychoanalysis started to study the psychology of fixation.[8] Freud was distracted by the significant and abundant discoveries of the first twenty years, but did not forget his interest in the psychology of the phenomena that constituted the cathartic theory.

In the three years following the evolving interest in the psychology of the phenomena which were the substance of his informative theory Freud wrote *The Totem and Taboo* (1912–1913) and *On Narcissism* (1914c). Those two works were revisions of two main conceptions in the cathartic theory: the Oedipus complex and the libido. He gave the Oedipus complex a new perspective from an alleged anthropological model, which explained the triangular structure of the Oedipus instead of using it to explain some of the psychical outcomes of family structures. He introduced the process of identification with the parent of the same gender as necessary for the "other" to be defined, thus the ego (*I*) completes the triangular structure. The paper on narcissism posited the libido in the midst of a serious "problematique": Do we have one libido that divides or two with one that extends beyond its source in the ego but regresses to it creating the state of narcissism? Does the libido explain psychical phenomena or is it something that needs explaining by examining the phenomenon of narcissism? This is when he *had* to assume a primary phase of narcissism which the libido and psychical interest originate from. Those two works shifted the emphasis from what the theory was explaining to the explanations that seem to need explaining. Better, psychoanalysis was changing from a theory which explains some psychical phenomena of the individual to a theory searching for the psychology of the concepts needed and used to do the explaining.

His next move was revising three most fundamental concepts in his informative theory: instincts (*Trieben*), repression, and the unconscious. The papers on those subjects were named by Strachey "Papers on Metapsychology," because Freud was planning to publish them with few others under the title "Preliminary to a Metapsychology." These papers do not deal with any of the economic, topographic, or dynamic aspects of their subject matter. They are actually preliminary to metapsychology because they deal with the psychology of their subject matter.[9] Besides, Freud was quite aware that he was until then building metapsychologies and he knew that to get to "a satisfactory general conception of neuropsychotic disturbances [it] is impossible if one cannot link it with clear assumptions about normal mental processes" (letter, May 25). Although the revision of the concept of the unconscious was the third in this major turning point in the development of psychoanalysis, it has all the attributes of being the real instigator of those revisions—as I will show later. However, the three revisions in their sequence were first *Trieben,* second repression, and third the unconscious.

Infantile sexuality and its role in symptom formation forced Freud to revise his concept of *Trieb,* because he recognized that *Trieben* generate a wide range of reactions that do not look like they originate from one sexuality. In the paper on *Vicissitudes of the Trieben* (1915c) Freud reiterated the main arguments he raised in the book on infantile sexuality (1905d) about their *somatic origin,* which could only be surmised from their aim (123). The gap that exists between the somatic source and its representation in the *Triebhaft* aim is where the vicissitudes are generated. He stipulated four vicissitudes: (1) reversal into its opposite (the seat of confusion of identifications), (2) turning round the person's own self (regression and narcissism), (3) repression, (4) sublimation (the transformations of infantile sexual components of sexuality into social ties and attitudes). *Trieben* were not anymore urges of specific objective, like in the bipolarity of sex vs. self-preservation. The somatic aspects that constitute the *Trieb,* making them felt as need. Hence, the aim of the need exposes the psychical that is embedded in their vicissitudes. In other word, *the psychology of the Trieb is the psychology of the transformation of the somatic into something of psychical nature.* However, the *Trieb* could fail in transforming into one of its vicissitudes properly. The outcome of that failure becomes the subject of repression.

Repression (1915d) was the second topic to be revised in those papers on the psychology of the basic concepts in the cathartic theory. Freud remained captive of this concept in a peculiar way. It was his first and most prolific concept behind the birth of the theory of psychoanalysis in its first phase. But in a gradual way he realized that repression is only one of several other mechanisms (defenses) that create the psychoneuroses. He concluded that, "Psychoanalytic observations of the transference neuroses, moreover, leads to conclude that repression is not a defensive mechanism which is present from the beginning, and that it cannot arise until a sharp cleavage has occurred between consciousness and the unconscious mental activity—that *the essence of repression lies simply in turning something away from consciousness and keeping it at a distance, from consciousness*" (Ibid., 147). This statement is clearly denoting that repression—as it was perceived in the theory of catharsis—does not create the unconscious but is a result of an unconscious process. Freud suggested the presence of a *primal repression* that has to happen first in order for repression and the rest of the defensive mechanisms to follow. Freud named the secondary repression repression proper. Thus, primal repression creates the material that need to be properly repressed and defended against by other means. Freud did not demote his "pet concept" to a secondary status, although after the revisions of the 1915–1920 repression had no significant place in the theory anymore.

In addition to this revision of the concept itself, two more notes are worth underlining: (1) "The process of repression was not to be regarded as an event which takes place *once*" (Ibid., 151). (2) "Repression becomes accessible to us only by deducting that mechanism from the *outcome* of the repression (Ibid., 154)." The theory of psychoanalysis has changed from a theory of forgetting and recovering the repressed and remembering it *to a theory of a process that creates the psychical from aconscious material*[10, 11, 12] *(the meaning of aconscious will come in revision of the concept of the unconscious).* Such repression is dynamically active and keeps sending its representation to the system conscious, giving us the opportunity to uncover it. Since repression is no longer accountable for all that is unconscious, and it is not a one-shot act, therefore the concept of the unconscious was due to a revision to fit in the new emerging theory, especially that repression is only one of the vicissitudes of the *Trieb*.

The most important and significant revision of the theory was the revision of the concept of the unconscious. Its significance is not just because of its centrality in the theory of psychoanalysis but because "somehow" clinical analysts showed very little appreciation (understanding) of the impact that revision had on the total theory, while the non-clinical analysts were the ones who comprehended and assimilated that revision very easily. Freud states early in his revision that "repression does not cover everything that is unconscious. The unconscious has a wider compass: the repressed is part of the unconscious" (1915e, 166). This statement would lead to a simple conclusion: there are other mechanisms other than repression that could create the unconscious; therefore there must be more than the one unconscious which have the same function of expelling something from consciousness. Freud, still using the terminology of the catharsis theory, explained this matter in terms of cathecting and decathecting ideas, affects, urges, etc., which are destined to become unconscious. But, we could and should explain those matters in non-libido terminology because the libido theory is informative in a primitive way and the concept of narcissism relegated it to an impractical conception of psychical processes. If and when one of those rejectionable matters has to be warded off from consciousness or is acceptable to be permitted to enter it, its nature has to change to fit the system that it will move to. In Freud's words: "The transition from system *Ucs.* to the system next to it is not affected through the making of a new registration but through the change in its state, an alteration in its cathexis" (Ibid., 180). For an idea to become conscious it has to be modified by the secondary process to fit in the system *Cs.* This is the main idea of the theory of dreams: the wish has to undergo changes—dream work—to form the manifest dream or the dream as we report it. For instance, when some forbidden memories about the patient's father were close to his consciousness, they were transformed into negative transference feeling toward the analyst. They were metonymically disguised, and entered consciousness in that way.

The system *Ucs.* in Freud's original topographical model (1900a) was depicted separately from the two systems, *Cs., Pcs.* The reason is that the latter two systems are made of material that is originally conscious and created by the rules of the secondary processes. The *Ucs.*, on the other hand, is structured according to the rules of the primary process. The unconsciouses that are not the product of repression must become formations of different nature. Freud resorted to an economical conception of the three psychical systems where he envisages the existence of power or struggles between the systems, leading to a dynamic balance between them decided by the strength of the "cathexes" of the issues in play. He stipulated that the unconscious is dynamically repressed, yet he admitted that it is not the strength of the repressed effect or idea that decides if it will become unconscious or not "because we have now gained the conviction that there are some latent ideas which do not penetrate consciousness, however strong they may have become" (1912g, 262). Those contradictions in the old theory of repression made him extricate a third type of unconsciousness and call it the systemic unconscious or system *Ucs.* (Ibid., 266). The *systemic* unconscious is unconsciousness that is neither caused by repression, nor created by another mechanism, but because it is a system that is qualitatively different; it is what he foresaw to be the product or primary repression. Differentiating the three meanings of the unconscious led to unearthing the very nature and characteristics of that system, which are—point in fact—the essence of anything psychoanalytic about the human subject and his psyche. It is a psychical system that does not conform to the conscious way of thinking because it has no sense of negation, time, or contradiction, and no limits to displacement or condensation (Matte-Blanco 1975). The characteristics of the systemic unconscious are what fascinated the thinkers, philosophers, artists, and the rest of the non-clinical analysts including the public in general, in the Western world.

Freud went back to this concept eight years later (1923b) to add that: "the *Ucs.* does not coincide with the repressed; it is true that all that is repressed is *Ucs.* [should have been unconscious] but not all that is *Ucs.* is repressed. A Part of the ego, too—and heaven knows how important a part—may be *Ucs.* . . . When we find ourselves thus confronted by the necessity of postulating a third *Ucs.*,which is not repressed . . . being unconscious begins to lose significance for us. It becomes a quality which can have many meanings, a quality which we are unable to make, as we should have hoped to do, the basis of far reaching and inevitable conclusions" (18). In hind sight, I could say that Freud knew all that had to be known about the unconscious from the time he worked out the problem of the dream in 1900, but he did not have the needed vocabulary to express all his views at the time. *Paying attention to infantile sexuality would have been impossible if he did not notice the working of the primary process in disguising aspects of childhood behaviors in adult sexuality, making them systemically unconscious in the psychoneuroses. Gradually he created ways to express his ideas like the economic and the systemic unconscious (Usc.), yet he remained captive of the informative concept of the unconscious. He could not make the leap to the process of unconsciousness in the human subject.* Freud left us a complete theory of the unconscious, which Lacan's major contribution was to define it as structured like a language (Lacan 1977c).

The revisions of 1915 changed psychoanalysis from a theory of the psychical phenomena that the individual lives in health and sickness to a theory of the psychology of human subject who embodies those processes. Better, *psychoanalysis changed from a psychological theory of the individual to a theory of the psychology of the phenomena that create the human subject (the actual individual in his uniqueness).*

Freud changed emphasis from a theory of the formation of dreams, sexual conflicts, psychopathology, the modalities of hysterical phantasies, to a theory of the psychology of the phenomena that are the components of the human subject, like the non-repressed unconscious, the variations the *Trieben* are capable of producing, and the process of changing a somatic stimulus into an affective attachment. The old informative theory was elementary in its information, and an ordinary person could read it and get from it exactly what a candidate in training could: information and knowledge of what analysts think about psychical matters. The new theory after the revisions still had information, but information regarding the subject matter of psychoanalysis—the human subject and not his psychological manifestations. Freud tried to address the psychology of several psychical phenomena that were previously used to explain the individual. He previously established the modality of the pleasure/reality principles to explain what happens to affect (the previously called psychical energy and libido). Based on the Bleuler notion about the bound and unbound affect, Freud developed the idea that when affect is bound it belongs to the reality principle and when unbound it remains the core of the pleasure principle. According to that he configured the concept of *Triebhaft* duality: sexual vs. self-preservation.

Based on the revision of the libido theory in the paper on narcissism he said: "The original opposition between the ego-instinct and the sexual-instincts proved to be inadequate. A portion of the ego-instinct was seen to be libidinal; sexual-instincts—probably along others—operated in the ego. . . . The distinction between the two kinds of instincts, which was originally regarded as in some sort of way *qualitative*, must now be characterized differently-namely as being *topographical*" (1920g, 52). Previous to that statement he said: "No knowledge would have been more valuable as the foundation for true psychological science than the approximate grasp of the common characteristics and possible distinctive features of instincts [*Trieben*]" (Ibid., 51). Accordingly, Freud looked for *Triebhaft* modality that could replace the sexual-ego modality. His insight led him to the more elementary and fundamental duality of life and death *Trieben* (we will get to that later). Going *Beyond the Pleasure Principle* was significant—but not a turning point—in the history of the informative theory of psychoanalysis.

Freud was keen to build psychoanalysis on the firm grounds of an informative theory. He always tried but his intuition and insights did not allow him to ignore that psychoanalysis is not a theory of the individual but a process of discovering the subject behind the individual. He tried one more time to have a final construction of his discoveries in his book *The Ego and the Id* (1923b) and hoped it to be—at least—a theoretical modality of psychoanalysis. In its original German it reads: the *I* and the *It* (almost the other). The English translation reified the pronouns to a degree that inadvertently created what was later called Ego Psychology. Freud divided the individual into three entities or agencies of distinct substance, the *I* representing the "aware subject" or the speaking individual, the *It* is the part of the subject that he is not aware of, and *super-I* or the identification with a narcissistic version of the *I* that is self-observing and critical of the difference between *I* and the narcissistic *I*. Anyhow, the oversimplification of the subject matter of psychoanalysis in this way has all the features of a desperate attempt at a final theoretical framework that would tabulate all the discoveries and conception of the theory. Nevertheless, Freud's intuition made him realize that for that modality to have any psychoanalytical meaning he had to presuppose the existence the three systems of *Cs.*, *Pcs.*, and *Ucs.*, within each of them. The new modality of the three agencies was void of any psychoanalytic meaning without the modality of the psychical systems of the topographical point of view.

Matte-Blanco (1975) shows how Freud was apologetic about *The Ego and the Id*. But there is no better proof to Freud's regret than saying about this work: "Now I am prepared to hear you ask me scornfully whether our ego-psychology comes down to nothing more than taking commonly used abstractions literally [reified] and in a crude sense, and transforming them from concepts into things by which not much would be gained" (1933a, 60). His reply to his remark that he only renamed things and did not come up with a new discovery is an apology and not an explanation. But the firm proof is his revision of the theory of anxiety (1926d) which pulls the rug from underneath the ego. In *Inhibitions, Symptoms and Anxiety*, Freud starts the work with an array of questions and unsatisfactory answers to end with two major conclusions: a role for anxiety in symptom formation and the need for a non-libidinal interpretation of anxiety. He concludes that anxiety is not the affective transformation of frustrated libido, but a reaction to the ego's inadequacy in dealing with danger, which is part of the phantasmic childhood of the psychoneurotic. He then examines the specific role of anxiety in symptom formation with emphasis on the obsessional neuroses showing that the choice of the defense mechanism is determined by the danger that provokes anxiety. He ends the book with a very significant revision to the concept of castration anxiety, saying that it is the anxiety about losing the love of the object and not the loss of the organ (penis). This revision puts the psychological meaning of the word castration in the place of its physical denotation, which makes more sense in light of the three revisions of 1915 and the timid revoking of ego-psychology. The revision could be extended to all other remaining "questionable" concepts like penis envy and Oedipal competitions. Literarily, the so-called structural point of view (the new topography of ego psychology) is good for a fictional psychology of the individual's psychodynamics but is not psychoanalysis or conducive to a psychoanalytic theory.

CONCLUSION

There must be dozens of ways to summarize fifty-seven years of work of a prolific thinker and writer like Freud. My approach was aimed at showing, through the revisions of the main concepts in the theory, that it was turning from an informative theory of the psychological manifestations of the individual into a theory of the psychology of the human subject. This means turning the informative theory of the individual into a structural theory, which suits the psychology of the human subject. To clarify this subtle difference we should emphasize that the content of the theory of the individual, as Freud and the pioneers suggested, was metaphors of the fundamentals of the human subject. To say that the individual's thoughts could be subjected to repression is a metaphor of expelling them from consciousness. This metaphor led to the metaphor of unconsciousness. Unconsciousness shed a light on different ways that thoughts could exist outside the subject's consciousness. Therefore, a new metaphor had to be created to connote the nature of that human phenomenon. The concept of narcissism came to account for the split in the subject's identity. Every time a new metaphor was needed to account for a human feature the theory changed our way of looking at the human subject, i.e., it opened our minds to attributes that needed to be investigated further and not just be mentioned. Freud used the *Id* (it) in his theory as a metaphor of four things, creating a great deal of confusion about the Ego, which is another metaphor that stands for a pronoun and not a "thing." Advancing psychoanalysis was not by arguing and a disagreeing on the adequacy of those metaphors or replacing them, but was to search for what the metaphor "represented" especially that we still have no precise idea of what is represented by those metaphors. The history of the informative theory was not purely the making of Freud's scientific endeavor but it had something to do with the politics of the psychoanalytic organization. Exploring that aspect would shed light on the contemporary theoretical shambles.

NOTES

1. Despite my doubts about the "solid information" I got from reading Freud, I noticed unmistakable differences in my work as a clinical psychologist. I was trained in interpreting psychodiagnostic tests as reflections of the patient's mental and emotional condition. After reading the psychoanalytic text the psychometric profiles became vivid looking into the psychological life of a person. A Minnesota Multiphasic Personality Inventory profile was not anymore reflecting a degree of depression or an elevation in somatization; it was a description of the patient in front of me managing his psychological life.

2. The Ottawa Freudian Group (1990–1994) was made up of eight permanent members and some casual and visiting colleagues. Four were psychologists with varied psychological background. The rest were philosophers, academicians, psychiatrists, sociologists, and nurses.

3. There were some brilliant contributions that Freud benefited from, but Freud was encyclopedic. He could be compared in general terms to Aristotle who was the first encyclopedic philosopher, in spite of the many misconceptions that were discovered centuries later in his works. Possibly, Freud's encyclopedic mind was the reason some of the great minds around him realized his ability to contribute to their endeavors and sought his friendship. Admiring Freud puts whatever he has done and achieved within the context of the circumstances of doing it. It also puts his work in the context of what has been achieved by others around him at the same period of time. Evaluating his work in the context of their circumstances reveals both the greatness of the work and the person.

4. In my opinion Adler and Jung's "desertion" of Freud was instigated by sensing the pending changes that he was about to introduce to psychoanalysis.

5. I am using Bion's terminology with almost the same connotation: psychoanalysis moved from sexuality as an urge to sexuality as the end result of the transformations of pleasure in different part of the body.

6. He started his paper on "'Wild' Psycho-analysis" (1910k) with warning against using psychoanalytic *information* as material for interpretation.

7. Freud was very clear about this point two years earlier in his paper on "'Wild' Psycho-analysis" (1910k).

8. It is important to note that Freud's ideas about the emergence of the psychical from the physical were already mentioned in his posthumously published "Project for a Scientific Psychology" (1950a).

9. Freud was puzzling much earlier about what to call his *psychology* (my italics) that leads beyond consciousness (Letter, March 10).

10. Unconscious denotes making something conscious "unconscioused." Primary repression deals with material that is not conscious, has no means to ever become conscious but sends representations to the conscious system. It is better to distinguish this state from the unconscious by calling it aconscious (see Fayek 2014).

11. Freud said: "One of the earliest and most important functions of the mental apparatus is to bind the instinctual impulses which impinges on it, to replace the primary process prevailing in them by the secondary process and convert their freely mobile cathected energy into mainly quiescent (tonic) cathexis" (1920g, 62).

12. Ego psychologists, especially in the United States, reversed Freud reifications and equated the *Id* with the unconscious and made it the reservoir of the instincts (misreading and misinterpreting Freud's exact text), and equating the Ego with consciousness and antithesis of the *Id*.

TWO

The Informative Theory and Theoretical Plurality

In a brief summary of the psychoanalytic situation from after World War I to the time Freud passed, Gaddini said (1984): "[that there were] many changes in the twenty years between the two wars, from the surprising reformulation of the theory of instincts (Freud 1920g) and the revolutionary structural theory (Freud 1923) to the recognition of the mechanisms of defense of the ego (A. Freud 1936), the transference and, the tacitly, the counter-transference, and in general the study of the theory of technique Fenichel (1941) . . . this is not to mention the compulsory institution of training" (13). This very condensed account of the situation before Freud's death highlights two things: (1) that Freud's structural metapsychology (ego psychology) was considered—by most analysts—his final rendering of the theory of psychoanalysis. (2) The psychoanalytic organization was mandated to overlook all matters pertaining to the future of psychoanalysis: theory, training, and practice.

The first point confirms Freud's incessant endeavor to formulate a theory of psychoanalysis in spite of his reluctance to bring it to a premature conclusion. His intuition was to safeguard against his disciples' fretfulness about final informative theory that would identify and define psychoanalysis. Although Freud would have wanted to consider his "structural" metapsychologies a final statement about psychoanalysis, he never acknowledged it to be (1933a; 1940a). The second point is rather difficult to deal with as one issue. The psychoanalytic organization and the training committee, in particular, relates to more than one aspect of psychoanalysis. Freud's definition of psychoanalysis (1923a) outlines the multiple functions of the psychoanalytic organization. We should examine the organization of psychoanalysis and its obvious role in creating the contemporary fragmentation of psychoanalysis as a first step.

Idealizing Freud and the formation of the secret committee were very important factors in saving the psychoanalytic movement from early fragmentation and in giving the theory a stable environment to evolve and transform. Freud, and psychoanalysis in general, benefited from the respect he owned because he was able to state his insights even before he firmly verified them. The secret committee, which did not keep its secrecy long, gave the ordinary membership a sense of continuation that was needed to keep it in line and not deviate prematurely from the classical doctrine. Eventually after establishing the system of training in 1922, the power and the special status enjoyed by the members of committee were transferred to the training committees. The International Training Committee established replicas in each regional training center in the world. The international training committee and the local training committees inherited the old structures of the secret committee with superficial modifications. Nonetheless, *those two features outlived their usefulness but did not dissipate*. The compulsion to maintain them as the modality of the psychoanalytic organization created an atmosphere of dissention among psychoanalysts because they were used to create false sense of continuity when continuity in the literal Freudian meaning is change and revisions, i.e., continuity became stagnation when the Freudian doctrine meant developing the theory.

Regardless of the flaws in the classical doctrine it was a breakthrough. It offered—for the first time—a view of the individual that has never been envisaged before in Western culture and the medical profession: the individual is not what he claims to be because he does not know everything about himself, but sometimes he reveals aspects of himself without being aware of that. The unconscious feature in the individual's existence fascinated the thinkers and intellectuals of all sorts, but constituted a problem to the medical profession: how to medicalize this feature, or how to integrate a non-medical aspect of the individual in his status as a patient (when he becomes one). The revelation that the individual is not really what he appears to be (intrinsically and not morally) had the major impact that Freud said "dethroned consciousness as the ultimate knowing function in the individual and shrunk Man's narcissism as Darwin did before." Psychoanalysis changed the social and the intellectual culture along with the medical profession by just removing the fixed illusions about the human being. The theory of psychoanalysis looked as if it would eventually find all the attributes of the individual—psychoanalysis becoming a complete informative theory of the individual.

We should at this point underscore an important difference between the previously formed theories of the individual like religious theory, social theory, etc., and the theory of psychoanalysis. Those theories did not talk about the individual's attributes as metaphors of his essence; they considered him to be what they thought of him (a sinner, a social animal, etc.). On the other hand, psychoanalysis unintentionally treated—and supposedly still does—the formulations of its findings as metaphors, i.e., concepts that require interpretation. In that sense, Freud metaphors of the individual's attributes were only the content of the theory of his time, which required and enabled us to search and research their equivalents in our time. He left us a methodology of thinking about the individual, a theoretical framework that is still open to more exploring, some very rich metaphors as a starter of a better ones, and both a subject-matter (the psychical aspects of the individual) that beckons us to look for a better subject matter (the psychology of the human subject). Narcissism, for instance, is a metaphor of the duality of the *I* and the *me* in the individual that leads to the human subject's intrinsic need for the *other* to maintain that duality. Ego, Id, and super-Ego are another metaphor of the possible internal failure of actualizing the self (which is a metaphor to be examined in future psychoanalysis).

Before Freud's death psychoanalysis was thriving as an international organization that also had a wide circle of followers in the intellectual fields. However, it was not "easy sailing" all the time. The psychoanalytic movement started as a promising theory of information about the psyche. But when Freud excluded or did not endorse what looked like final new contents provided by some mavericks, they dissented. He insisted that theory had not yet reached the core of the discovery. I will mention few of those crises briefly to emphasize that if psychoanalysis was merely another informative theory the disagreements it created and still creates should have been brief and passing, but they were not. They were unusually long lasting, involved splits with no separation, thus maintaining tension within the institution and building personal grudges and establishing divergent loyalties. The disagreements were all acrimonious, and would not have been taken personally by serious mature advocates if they were merely differences of opinion. But those conflicts were all lived within the psychoanalytic organization and involved competitions for positions on the different committees and subcommittees of the organization. Rangell (2004) described some of the personal ambitions of two particular "senior" analysts in regard to becoming presidents of the IPA and how their success and failure had a major role in accepting theoretical plurality as a principle. The theory of psychoanalysis as an informative theory created objective and subjective convictions that are very difficult to separate from the analyst's own personality and narcissism.

The first crisis was the breakup in the Vienna group between 1910 and 1913. It is known that Freud was not comfortable dealing with Adler for personality differences, but it was also because of major theoretical disagreements. The Freudian doctrine at that time was searching for the causes of the psychoneuroses, and he suggested that symptoms are expressions of failure in coping with sexuality. He also believed that infantile sexuality has not been explored enough and could hold the key to many of the emerging questions about the psychoneuroses. Adler, on the other hand, dismissed the centrality of psycho-sexuality in psychopathology, put the emphasis on the social factors and the struggle for significance, and rejected the intrapsychical as the core of the neuroses. Adler believed that he has come to discover the real and better causes of the psychoneuroses, when Freud considered his suggested etiology of sexuality was merely a temporary point in the development of the theory. It could be said—and it was said—that Freud did not tolerate disagreements but what Adler was proposing was an early foreclosure on the theory by offering the final word on causation, when Freud was convinced that psychoanalysis was at an early stage in its development. He was sincere in rejecting Adler's proposition and was not playing a game of "up-man-ship." Freud was justified to let go of Adler.

Jung too had formulated his theory of psychoanalysis on *phylogenetic* concepts like the collective unconscious, the archetypes, the usage of mythology and symbolic interpretation in the workings of dreams and symptom formation. Freud was impressed by Jung's discoveries and the speculative nature of the collective unconscious and the archetypes of human thinking. Jung—to him—was making great contribution to the understanding of the primary process, its basis, permutation in our waking and healthy life, and its contribution to understanding the genesis of psychical life. However, Freud's theory comprised *genetic* as well as *phylogenetic* explanations of the psychoneuroses. Jung did not take well to the genetic origin of the psychoneuroses and preferred to resign from the presidency of the IPA in 1913 to establish his own school of psychoanalysis. This could be taken as upstaging Freud with a different theory, but Freud's efforts to keep Jung in the main stream of psychoanalysis proves that he did not see it that way.

Although Freud recognized both the genetic and the phylogenetic factors in his theory, he did not see them as theoretical explanations because he insightfully realized that they still lurked in the background of what is particular in the individual's experiences, therefore cannot be taken as "absolutes" that could formulate theories. His major attribution of the "phylogenetic" to psychological life is circumscribed to the working of phantasies (Draft M, 1897a, 1916–1917). He suggested the existence of four primary phantasies that are phylogenetically founded and form the modality of our whole phantasy life, which is individually constructed. Once again we can see that Freud's disagreement with Jung was personal on the surface but it was a result of a fundamental difference about the theory that was continuing to change and defied foreclosure. The phylogenetic would not be considered a constituent of the psychology of the individual but as a formative aspect of the individual's psychical life.

Once the two early crises were passed there were no problems for quite some time. Analysts were following the main drift of Freud's new endeavor: researching the psychical phenomena more and avoiding premature foreclosures on its findings. When the principle of mandatory training was adopted in the 1920s, making it a precondition for membership in the IPA, homogeneity in the population of psychoanalysts lessened the disagreements among them. This was an advantageous development resulting in enriching the literature with some very creative new ideas, and openness to add new and significant ideas the informative theory. *It seems that institutional stability allowed more theoretical freedom.* The new attitude attracted the attention of quite a number of thinkers, artists, and philosophers who participated enthusiastically in the psychoanalytic movement in different counties and professions like L. Binswanger the Swiss psychiatrist and psychotherapist, Rollo May the American psychologist and thinker, William James the American psychologist and philosopher who invited Freud to the United States in 1909, etc.

In other words, after the war of 1914–1918, there was a flood of important thoughtful discoveries by clinical psychoanalysts, supported by outstanding contributions from the non-clinical "intelligentsia" in the area of human nature. The secret committee disbanded and the training committee usurped its power, analysts were occupied with their theory and there were more glorious things for psychoanalysts to get busy with, than bickering about the imperfections of the theory of catharsis.

Notwithstanding all that advancement in the status of psychoanalysis, some of the original disciples felt left behind because of the new and strong changes in the informative theory. Psychoanalysis was moving more toward a structural theory; a *theory of how things happen in* the human subject. They remained preoccupied with the limited sphere of a theory of *what and why*. They mainly saw it fit to question the Freudian protocols of practice and suggested doing away with some of its basics for the sake of brevity. They also questioned the objective of psychoanalyzing, and came up with different perspectives of improving the classical theory (Alexander and French 1946; Fenichel 1953; Ferenczi 1952; Rank 1968; and Reich 1945). Two main things could be learned from those calls for improvement: (1) They did not understand the organic and fundamental link between a theory of the unconscious and the analysis of the unconscious; analyzing the unconscious dictates no short cuts. (2) Psychoanalyzing is not informing the analyzed about his unconscious; it is leading him toward it for him to learn about it. Freud's clinical protocol was an integral part of his ongoing theoretical evolution, i.e., to accept the theory means to accept the clinical protocol. In any case, most of the arguments around those issues were colored by some personal conflicts and they did not live long after those analysts passed.

The history of the psychoanalytic movement is surprising when we consider the objective of the secret committee. It came as a result of the disintegration of the early group of analysts that surrounded Freud and the major threat to the newly formed International Psychoanalytic Association after Jung's resignation. The committee was meant to protect psychoanalysis by unifying it under the banner of the orthodoxy of the Freudian doctrine, arguing and defending its purity, barring the deviant analysts from continuing their affiliation to the association; it was a group of analysts who were presumably mostly alike and closely similar in their views and understanding of the theory and its practice. Moreover, they were to protect Freud by their unity. The history of the committee shows something else which is significant in understanding the nature of the psychoanalytic institution since its inception. The committee lost its secrecy very quickly and was recognized as a special group of analysts who were the closest to Freud. Not only the demeanor of its members reflected the extra narcissistic status they enjoyed, but Freud too made that publicly known in more than one occasion. The bickering and tensions between the members of the committee—though a little quieter than among the rest of the analytic community—never stopped. The committee eventually revealed that it was serving another function that was unconscious to its own members: the committee was to protect its members from deviating and disbanding as the early group did. They did not form a bodyguard to Freud; on the contrary Freud's presence in their midst kept them together for a time, while they were continuing the bickering and forming internal allegiances. I am not mentioning this historical fact to snicker, but to underline a characteristic in the psychoanalytic organization: although the committee claimed to be serving a noble purpose like maintaining high standards of psychoanalytic practice, it was unconsciously serving another quasi-noble objective of maintaining a cohesive body of unified analysts. *We should not be missing that contemporary institutions are doing the same thing*. The committee eventually disbanded in 1927 (Jones 1957) with Abraham's death, Rank's "outrageous" ideas and behaviors, and Ferenczi's delayed transference reaction to Freud.

We could—for now—accept that the crises in psychoanalysis were caused by more than what deceptively seem as neurotic, narcissistic, and power struggle spats between individual analysts. There were also real disagreements about the theory. We should ask: What is the problem with psychoanalytic theory that makes the disagreement about it turn into personal conflicts, and keep creating and repeating the same condition until now? The immediate but unsatisfactory answer is that if psychoanalysis is a theory of what and why (cause-effect theory) it will be an informative theory, thus some analysts would aspire to conceive of better causes to replace the original one.[1] A slightly better answer is that a functional theory in the humanities communicates information about complex phenomena, which could bear more than one causal explanation.

THE ORGANIZATION OF PSYCHOANALYSIS AFTER FREUD

Right after Freud's death there were already indications of disgruntlements in the regional psychoanalytic societies in some countries (England, France, and later but in a different style in the United States). As I know—from some second-hand information about some of those early events, and later by witnessing them in three different organizations—that each society had an "undeclared" group of analysts (training analysts) who quietly assumed the function of the secret committee through being the permanent members of the training committees in their societies. First, the old pattern of a secret committee disguised as the training committee was adopted in all the regional national societies. This was part of the pattern inherited from the old organization that inherited the Freudian authority. It was not difficult at the beginning to accept that because there were still first generation psychoanalysts continuing what they were doing before. They had the authority to select the future membership in their society through the mandatory training that all new members had to undergo.

Freud's approval of forming the secret committee made it a tradition to have members of such committees who assume special status in the organization psychoanalysis. Shortly after Freud's death major crises were initiated—indirectly—by members of the training committees, using their previous supervisees and candidates to support their claimed distinguished position in the organization. As Freud saw in the committee a lasting organizational structure that should continue after him and after the life of its members, in order to preserve its objective of defending his legacy and the purity of psychoanalysis, the members of that committee became leaders of psychoanalysis. In most, if not all, the societies and institutes there were mini-committees of a "quiet" group of analysts who controlled training, the different sub-committees, and the selection and sometimes the election of candidates to membership in the societies. They also controlled the publication venues and preserved themselves and their cronies the first right to publish. There were always powerful elite in the societies and the institutes. They inherited their privileges by being close to the previous powerful group. The rest of the membership, as tradition dictated, was more or less thankful for being accepted in the society of psychoanalysis. They quietly accepted the split between the privileged and the average either by residual unresolved transferences, the aspiration to be selected to some sub-committee, or the hope of taking the place of the retiring members of the silent groups. This is the political background of psychoanalysis after Freud's death, and in different degrees in the different societies until now. To be specific, when Freud died the psychoanalytic societies and institutes were headed by ego psychologists—very devoted ones. Anna Freud was in England, Sacha Nacht in France, and Heinz Hartmann was in the United States. But the grains of revolt were also there represented by Klein in England, Lacan in France, and the Colombia group in the United States. The theory evolved for the last seventy years or so in that political atmosphere.

Until the end of WWI psychoanalysis was concentrating on the patients who were diagnosed with hysteria (conversion and anxiety) and phobias. I would also add the obsessive compulsion neuroses (the Rat Man). In the twenty years between the two world wars, Freud's two main later works on instincts and the structure of the ego became landmarks of a new psychology, i.e., ego psychology. This psychology was officially launched by Anna Freud in 1936. It became a trend to use her suggested system of defenses in explaining any type of psychopathologies. Gaddini (1984) took a very interesting angle to condense a new line of theoretical evolution, which was the change in the psychopathology that psychoanalysis was dealing with in each period of that evolution. He noted that after the second war analysts expanded the spectrum of the psychopathologies they dealt with. This expansion is worth examining. The burgeoning fascination with the dynamics of the transference-counter transference phenomenon, Reich's interest in character formation (1945), and the beginning of interest in the place of narcissism in psychopathology expanded the scope of psychoanalysis beyond expectations. It is debatable if the expansion was a result of more clinical sophistication in differential diagnosis or freeing the theory from the limitations of ego psychology. However, the new additions to the informative theory, tempting as they were, opened a frontier that was never envisaged to become part of the psychoanalytic lot.

The changes started to happen between the two wars when Freud was still around, yet they were neither considered deviations from his doctrine nor explications of the traditional conceptions. Therefore they did not raise much debate, and no one expected any trouble with them. However, there were some signs portending the emergence of crises in the three regional societies of Britain, France, and the U.S. association. On the surface they all looked like personal conflicts and competitions, but in principal they were the "growing pains" of an evolving informative theory, which inevitably created a cloudy political atmosphere. We learned from the history of crises in psychoanalysis that discerning theoretical disagreement from personal conflicts is not a straightforward affair.

In Britain a crisis started with an unofficial declaration of personal conflict between Anna Freud and Melanie Klein over the domination of the society. Officially they both claimed fundamental theoretical differences. The gest of it was A. Freud's insistence on ego psychology as the last Freudian theoretical formulation of the intrapsychical, while Klein found in child analysis more basic and foundational explanations of adult intrapsychical psychodynamics. She moved the points of interest from the varied forms of psychopathology to the mother-child relationship and what is involved in it. It was a major theoretical disagreement which divided the society and threatened the institution of training. However bitter and unrelenting the disagreements, the British found "a negotiated solution" in creating three groups under the same "union Flag." The conflict was averted; the institute and training were saved, because an agreement was reached to preserve the society and its institute without giving up the theoretical stand taken by the analysts or the candidates.

However clear the personal conflict between the two strong ladies of psychoanalysis was, we cannot overlook the fact that the theoretical divide in Britain remained very much alive after both antagonists died. It even got wider and spread over the whole of the IPA organizations, proving the seriousness of the split between the intrapsychic and the interpersonal stands in psychoanalysis. The Freud–Klein spat was not just personal dislikes or competition over the domination of the organization; it is clear now that their theoretical differences were real in spite of using them to disguise political rifts. The Freud–Klein conflict was the first sign of dissatisfaction with ego psychology as a theory of psychoanalysis, because we will see the same thing happening in the "French Splits," and later in the American psychoanalytic diversities.

We cannot say that what happened in the United States in the late 1960s and the 1970s were just matters of loyalties to the memory of the two leading lady analysts. What happened in *Controversies* was prototypical of what happened all along in the evolution of psychoanalysis. Contrary to an affinity to psychologizing conflict in the psychoanalytic movement, all serious conflicts were cloaked in personal likes and dislikes, when they were always theoretical conflicts. The theory of psychoanalysis has the predisposition to create controversies.

Psychoanalysis came to France a little late, although Marie Bonaparte, who was an influential person in the French society, had her analysis with Freud in Vienna quite earlier. The French medical profession and the cultural circles in Paris were not eager to learn about Freud and psychoanalysis because they believed that what they have was superior to what he offered. However, by 1920, a few physicians read Freud and opened the door of Paris for psychoanalysis to gradually attract the attention of the elite intellectual community. We have to keep in mind that before WWII that community was—in more than one way—more sophisticated than any other in the other capitals in Europe. There was a good mix of thinkers, artists, writers, psychologists, psychiatrists, etc., who were in true lively cultural integration.

The few analysts who managed to read Freud in the 1920s were able to start forming the Paris Psychoanalytic Society in 1926 and its institute in 1934. The society was very much under the influence of Hartman and the Loewenstein, and the official school of psychoanalysis in France at that time was ego psychology. They were the two analysts who championed the splits from main stream psychoanalysis later: *Lagache and La-*

can. After WWII the society and the institute continued to grow and resume their activities. Nacht was sort of more official in following the "party line" while Lacan and Lagache were typical French intellectuals before and beyond being analysts. Ego psychology did not seem to satisfy their growing interest in the Freudian text. It could help to mention that the few analysts who read Freud in the 1920s accepted his method of treatment but had reservations about his theory. Therefore, Lagache, Lacan, and some others disagreed with Nacht's rigid and narrowed views on training. They split forming the Paris Psychoanalytic Society. The main undeclared disagreement was about the input in the theory from outside the limited resources of the classical clinical French psychoanalysts. Lacan got his starting idea of the mirror stage from the inspiring H. Wallon (an outstanding child psychologist). Lagache was an academic psychologist with a wide scope of knowledge about the place of psychoanalysis in the general theory of psychology. Those two with their followers caused the first split. But Lacan's controversial and dubious ideas about the practice forced him to split from the French Association to form his society "L'Ecole Freudienne" which was not recognized by the IPA but had tremendous success among analysts of all walks. This society kept splitting after his death, and maybe is still splitting now.

The splits in France were once again initiated by the official authority's insistence on the preservation of ego psychology as the "official" theory of psychoanalysis. Breaking away from that rigidity had to take the form of a rebellion. Ego psychology—once again—was the straw that broke the society's back, but this time the revolt was in the French style: less inclination to compromise, deep sense of richness of culture around, propensity to speculate and philosophize, and most of all a natural sense of being different without being hostile. In more than one way, this attitude gave psychoanalysis in France bigger latitudes to create a psychoanalytic culture. Although the Kleinian camp produced major psychoanalytic minds, French psychoanalysis created a remarkable formative school of psychoanalysis.[2]

The history of psychoanalysis in the United States starts with a split from the IPA, because in 1938 the American Association put conditions to keep its affiliation to the IPA. The pressure of the medical profession dictated that for psychoanalysis to be accepted as a profession of treatment, it has to restrict its membership to medical graduates. Therefore, the "American" asked for a special membership status in the IPA. The result was limiting the role of the international organization in the internal affairs of the "American," in regard to training and membership. Because of WWII the matter did not seem to be significantly alarming, added that after the years of the war psychoanalysis in Europe was almost dead. A large number of European analysts moved to the United States before and after the war, a fact that made "the American" the only active organization of psychoanalysis for many years and was actually the psychoanalytic "Marshall plan" of psychoanalysis in Europe and the rest of the world.

Yet, right after the war splits appeared in New York—Colombia, Baltimore, Washington, and Philadelphia, then moved to the West Coast, in particular Los Angeles. However, the actual splitting was limited to small groups of analysts. The reasons for those splits are extensive and complex to give their details or to make sense of them. Rangell (2004) is of the opinion—based mainly on anecdotal events—that the main factor behind them was personal likes and dislikes (neurotic squabbles), a position taken by Freud regarding the splits of his time. Eisold (1994) gave it a psychoanalytic explanation centered on the practice of psychoanalysis, the anxieties that accompany it, and defensive measures against those anxieties. The splits in the United States were very much related to the two issues that swept the analytic community in Europe: ego psychology and the hegemony of the training committees, i.e., the heirs of the secret committee that wanted to force ego psychology as the only theory of psychoanalysis.

In the eastern United States the conflict was the emergence of some liberal and very gifted psychoanalysts who wanted to introduce their views about matters that pertain to rigid interpretations of Hartmann's ego psychology, and to widen the scope of both the subject matter of psychoanalysis and the methodology of psychoanalytic observations. Those changes not only challenged ego psychology, they encouraged and inspired interest in topics ranging from infant observation to social morality. In fact, some new thoughts about technique were visited and challenged, especially by Fenichel and Alexander who presented two distinctively different outlooks on therapy. However, in hindsight, the splits in the East Coast were about the very fundamental basis of intrapsychical and the interpersonal points of view though they were disguised in accusations of deviating from the classical doctrine. Critiquing ego psychology or questioning Hartmann's ideas was not tolerated and was silenced by condemning dissenters as deviating from the classical doctrine. The situation was so important to the American that Anna Freud was invited to get involved in the United States supporting ego psychology and warning against the impending invasion of Klein to North America.

On the West coast, the same acrimony started but in a less civilized way especially when Bion moved there. The American Association and The International Association were called upon to mediate and find a solution to the right to obstruct a psychoanalytic theory and its supporters from having their own preferences. The matter almost reached a foreboding legal level at a certain stage of the conflict, when the lawsuit of 1988 gave the right to non-medical people to train and become members of the "American Association." If anything, this lawsuit is a good "peeping hole" on the internal dynamics of the politics in psychoanalysis. It proved that the analytic organization is confused about its function, objectives, and duties.

The history of the splits in those three societies is full of anecdotal evidence that support the strong belief in the personal factor, mainly narcissistic. However, it is not reasonable to imagine that the 1950s and 1960s were years of *a neurotic epidemic* that swept all the psychoanalytic organizations in the world. There are several "psychoanalytic explanations" to the dynamics of the psychoanalytic organization, ranging from the model of the *Totem and Taboo* to Limentani's remarkable comment (1974) that training analysis might be antithetical to analysis. Those explanations are dangerous, because they could be right after all, and would stop us from looking for their impersonal side, which is also equally important. To put it in another way: ego psychologists after Freud's death (maybe even before) took over steering of IPA, and the national branches in most countries. As the heirs of Freud's last theory they rejected any deviation from it, although in all likelihood if Freud lived longer he would have advocated changes to that theory. Other analysts had Freud's basic spirit and wanted to advance beyond the point he reached. They wanted to pass over the informative theory, build the structural theory of psychoanalysis, and move on. Their attempts were not permitted and their endeavors were thwarted. One could say that frustrating those members who wanted to continue Freud's tradition of advancing the theory were forced to get personal and even become neurotic in their fight for continuing the psychoanalytic journey. Each group of analysts in each society who "struggled" against the restrictions put on their ambitions, and dealt with the situation in their own personal and national temperament.

THE ORGANIZATION OF PSYCHOANALYSIS AND THEORETICAL PLURALITY

Wallerstein, as president of the IPA, admitted and approved of psychoanalytic theoretical plurality (the meeting of the international organization in Montreal, 1989). Advocating this idea was linked to two more beliefs: there are common grounds in our practice that unify us despite the apparent theoretical diversity, and eventually we will come back to a singular theory emanating from the clinical experience of psychoanalysts. The problem with that vision of the status of psychoanalysis at that time was that it was not asking two very pertinent questions: psychoanalysis was a singular theory, how did it become multiple theories? If it has become multiple theories what is specific about practicing that will unite them in the future? In other terms: if the psychoanalytic organization condones theoretical plurality now what did it do to avoid that situation in the first place and what would motivate it to restitute it?

The politics of the psychoanalytic organization, after Freud's death, succeeded in positioning an ego psychologist on the top of its main national branches, seemingly and wrongly so, to create stability and continuation. The plan backfired because it went against the true nature of the theory of psychoanalysis, which is to progress to more advanced points in understanding the "human subject." It is ludicrous to think now that the metaphor of the individual, as depicted in the structural point of view, would have allowed anything of value to contribute to his understanding. The gist of the individual in this "final theory" of Freud's is that the individual is a final configuration of urges and counter urges, that result in a psychodynamic structure of conflicting agencies (ego, super ego, and id). Hence, it is a theory of catharsis after all, that takes cover under a thin layer of a new metaphor of structures. The cathartic theory is informative by definition: it is not difficult not to see in the final configuration of the theory definitive information to adopt.

The ego as a metaphor of the individual would not have satisfied the competent psychoanalysts who were sprouting out in all societies and were capable of advancing psychoanalysis to new frontiers. Winnicott and Bion, Lacan and his followers, Laplanche and his colleagues, the school of the Menninger analysts, several others in South America, and the rest of Europe would not have and did not stand for the simplistic ideas of ego psychology. The thinkers who examined and explored psychoanalysis well acknowledged its great potential, but not its structural theory. The result was an unexpected situation created by the IPA: splits from the official organization, avowed rejections of ego psychology as the only theory of psychoanalysis, waves of critiques of the classical doctrine came from within the official organization. Those critiques with whatever theoretical replacement informative theories they offered were called schools of psychoanalysis; not because their initiators did not split from the IPA, but because the organization condoned the criticisms and accepted tampering with the theory. The IPA's situation got gradually worse because the critique of the classical doctrine reached a point where it became ethically unacceptable to consider those schools psychoanalytic when there was no criterion for psychoanalysis anymore. The conflict between the organization and the psychoanalysts was about what Ricoeur foresaw (1970). Ricoeur wondered if the IPA would incorporate the new advancement in psychoanalysis or try to stifle it, thus they have to infiltrate the theory from outside?

This point is especially important: when the organization had a firm grip on the membership and believed that they are supporting Freud's final theoretical formulation, there were concerns about the splitting of those whom they thought were just a few uncompliant members. In time, more members of the organization became critical of the indelible theory of catharsis and the structural view point of the individual. Instead of suggesting a review of the theory to address what proved to be valid discontentment, the IPA allowed a chaotic tampering and changing of the theory to take place, and called them schools of psychoanalysis. In a more direct explanation: the organization did not show concern about psychoanalysis, nor did it care about the psychoanalysts who were deviating from their theory and distorting it; *the organization cared for the organization and its continuance.*

Psychoanalysis took a dive from then on. In 1995, the IPA had formed a committee to study *The Crisis of Psychoanalysis* (Cesio 1995). The report of the committee started by saying: "A plague such as the one we psychoanalysts are facing today is a pandemia comparable to the one that descended on Thebes because of the murder of Laius, the father. And now: could it be the result of the murder of Freud, the father? Will we not discover, like Oedipus, that we ourselves are the murderers?" (2). The report confirmed in more than one way the existence of a crisis that is basically a crisis of the identity of psychoanalysis and the psychoanalysts. The manifestation of that crisis was an increasing deterioration of the attitudes toward psychoanalysis in the population of patients and the new professionals who would and could aspire to become analysts. What was more alarming is the obvious confusion and failure to make a diagnosis of the crisis let alone suggesting solutions for it. I will present just one part of the aforementioned report on the crisis written by a well-respected analyst which shows that the IPA is concerned about its survival more than the survival of psychoanalysis.[3]

Freedman (1995) concluded in the report that there are four problems behind the crisis (32–36) and suggested their remedies. He mentioned the difficulty contemporary analysts have with the classical doctrine. However, he did not address the possibility of a link between the demise of the theory and the crisis. I quote the four points he delineated of the crisis and italicize the remedies he suggested, underlining the particular difficulty or contradiction in his suggestions:

1. The crisis is inherent in the loss of our root identity, *and the remedy is to incorporate all new points of view* [plurality]. It is paradoxical to regain the root psychoanalytic identity by incorporating other identities. What preceded and caused our current identity crisis was the passive acceptance of theoretical plurality and the attempts at incorporating them in one psychoanalysis.

2. The crisis is inherent in the structure of analytic education, which is characterized by rigidity and inflexibility. His suggested *being more creative and allowing some leniency in training for less stringent psychoanalysis.* According to the IPA report, to which Freedman is a contributor, this leniency is already practiced, and resulted in serious "deviations in the teaching of its theory [psychoanalysis]. . . . In some institutes . . . there is such estrangement from the basics of psychoanalysis that *The Interpretation of Dreams* isn't studied" (Cesio 1995, 3–4). Freedman's remedy was itself the disease.

3. The crisis is inherent in the failure to acknowledge new social realities, *and the remedy is to accept new modalities of psychotherapy to accommodate different economic and ethnic factors.* Accommodating new modalities contributed, forcefully, to the loss and confusion about our psychoanalytic identity. It created the circumstance to lose the credibility of psychoanalysis as a distinct theory, mostly the credibility of the newly trained analysts. The "new social realities" he mentioned are not new to psychoanalysis, and they did not constitute a problem of any sort in the past. The economic factor is a nonstarter because the world now is in an affluent stage, and money is not a problem to most of those who need psychoanalysis and used to seek it. Analysis has proven itself before and is still a central ideological factor worldwide. It is in a better position to reoccupy its place in the fields of therapy and culture in the second half of the twentieth century, and the twenty-first century, than it was in the first half of last century. It is still better received in many places in the world, where it kept its identity, but less so in the parts of world that accommodated other modalities. In another part of the summary, Freedman (1995) contradicted himself by saying, "Some members note that our treatment approaches have often become too superficial in the effort to suit social adaptations or to fit statistical models" (33). This statement conflicts with what he stipulated about accepting new modalities of psychotherapy.

4. The crisis is inherent in the erosion of public trust and support, *and the remedy is to research to prove the viability of psychoanalysis and its effectiveness.* The remedy suggested has been tried before (Firestein 1978; Goldberg 1978; Wallenstein 1986), and was not conducive to gaining that confidence. It is difficult to fathom how we could present respectable research to prove the effectiveness of psychoanalysis when we have more than one psychoanalysis. If there is one psychoanalysis it would be, according to him, without a defining identity. Even worse, as Gedo (1999) said, "The cumulative published evidence has rendered the position some regarded as classical untenable. In the real world of clinical practice, in the vast majority of cases, the procedure of psychoanalytic mainstream proved to be inadequate, and the mainstream responded by shifting course. . . . Nor have the adherents of any of the other schools of psychoanalysis outside the American mainstream validated their claims of superior results" (31).[4]

Considering what was said in the report about the poor training and formation of contemporary analysts, we should ask *whether the erosion of public trust comes from the deterioration of psychoanalysis or the deterioration of psychoanalysts.* Orgel relates the crisis in its totality to the poor personal analysis of contemporary psychoanalysts, implying that the crisis is created by some sort of group neurosis in the membership. She says (1990): "I believe the narcissistic issues and aggressive countertransference of analysts of a generation ago were less well analyzed by *their* analysts than they are today (10) . . . the clinical analytic situation for scientific research depends on the competence of the analyst" (16). Eisold (2007) supports the notion that the crisis is mainly caused by the analysts. However, he looks at it from the angle of the isolation of the analyst and his distance from the population of the regular patient. From personal experience I would say that the preoccupation with the primacy of clinical practice over anything else in psychoanalysis comes from analysts who are less versed or interested in the theory and usually are inept to argue theoretical issues. Their concerns are limited and pertain to the profession of psychoanalysis and not to psychoanalysis, as such. This is an aspect in the crisis of psychoanalysis that is seldom dealt with in its concrete form: Are we facing a crisis about psychoanalysis or about the declining credibility of our practice? Could there be a relationship between the analyst's clinical competence and his theoretical prowess? In the mid-1970s, when metapsychology was considered unessential to the theory of psychoanalysis, G. Klein (1976)[5] advocated the development of a *clinical* theory, which would be all that a practicing psychoanalyst needs. This premise was accepted easily, and sometimes enthusiastically, as the best way to get rid of metapsychology once and for all. It also promised, indirectly, to elevate psychoanalysis to a reputable profession belonging to the medical field. This point of view was Wallerstein's solution to the problems created by theoretical plurality, and his conviction that we have common clinical grounds that could substitute for a theory of psychoanalysis (1988; 1990). *Professions do not have theories of practice separate from their body of knowledge.* There is no clinical theory of medical practice, no theory of practice in architecture, civil engineering, or even law. A clinical theory of psychoanalysis is not, and would not be more, than what Freud recommended in his papers on technique (1912b; 1912c; 1913c): free association and interpretation.

The distinction between the theory and the practice of psychoanalysis is vital in discussing future psychoanalysis for many reasons. I will mention only one now. Future psychoanalysis is more likely to be a seriously shared endeavor of several professions that are not all involved in psychotherapy. In addition, some psychoanalysts might prefer to use psychoanalysis in other fields of interest (education, politics, social change, etc.). Therefore, we should address this problem to avoid it in the future when we have to move to the future without the burden of an unresolved crisis. The advocates of separating theory from practice (Klein 1976; Orgel 1990; Wallerstein 1988; 1990) did not address or discuss the issue; they just opted to what they thought to be a solution to their theoretical proclivities. There is no mention in the literature of the part played by each of the two contributing factors in the problem. The reason is that the IPA still refrains from evaluating the contemporary schools of psychoanalysis. There are two issues to address in evaluating contemporary psychoanalyses: tampering with the classical theory is not a way to overcome its shortcomings, because the theory has to be accepted or rejected as a whole. In the first case the classical theory has to be reconfigured, not just modified, by adding or getting rid of some of its concepts. The Freudian doctrine was and still is a dialectical enterprise that evolved—via continuous engagement between the theses and antitheses it uncovered—and within the framework of the centrality of the *Ucs.* in it (the intrapsychic). Therefore, anything else that is forced on the theory like intersubjectivity creates a new theory that has to have a subject matter that fits it. The second issue is that it is a theory, which is either accepted as a dialectical entity or rejected as an informative theory. In case of accepting it the dialectical basis of its informative theory would be the incentive to go beyond it to its structural base. Rejecting it would have one meaning only—the replacement theory should not usurp the designation of psychoanalysis because any replacement for the rejected theory of psychoanalysis will not be psychoanalysis and should claim another name.

It does not take much to realize that present-day psychoanalysis is stunted, but we need to seriously consider three issues in this regard: is this due to the IPA's negligence of the deterioration of the informative theory, or a result of allowing haphazard tampering with that theory with no firm policy on how much of that is permitted, or the quasi-compliant link between the training committees and the executive committees in the local and national psychoanalytic societies. To understand the crisis in psychoanalysis from this angle, we need to examine the nature of the informative theory more because we should be sure that the theory has no further future and not to expect results. The informative theory should lead us to its structural theory, because that theory could become future psychoanalysis.

NOTES

1. Freud was interested and even preoccupied with such a final informative theory of the psyche, but he was always able to break away from the temptation to be satisfied with any of his several "final" formats of a theory.

2. A formative theory of psychoanalysis is supposed to provide other branches of knowledge with a system of thinking which makes them all work on the same subject matter in the same way.

3. Twenty years after this report, none of its recommendations was discussed further, and we are in a worse condition now than before.

4. See chapter 6.

5. In the 1970s some analysts in the United States advocated the elimination of metapsychology from psychoanalytic theory, the adoption of other theoretical modalities like communication theory to be the explanatory framework of psychoanalytic work, and to formulate a theory of practice to be the only theory of psychoanalysis. Their literature shows the reasons for the failure of their attempts.

THREE

The Structural Base of Informative Theory

The important and significant informative theories guide other theorists to their structural bases by revealing new information which was difficult to miss or ignore. Copernicus's heliocentric theory revealed that all the planets (in the solar system) orbit the sun. The new information replaced the Euclidian chaotic model of the universe (as was seen at that time). The circular orbiting suggested by Copernicus was correct but not exact. The correctness of the rotations of the planets and the incorrectness of their orbiting proved to Kepler that Copernicus's theory was structurally sound. He worked on the orbits and their correct trajectories to discover that they orbit the sun in elliptic trajectories and not circular ones. Kepler's trajectories were informatively correct, but without a structural explanation of their elliptical course. Newton deduced the laws that determine those rotations, and concluded that gravity is the force behind them. Thus, gravity became the structural core of heliocentric theory, which in turn became the theory of the structure of the universe. The rest of the story is in what amazes us now, the two results of that sequence of events: relativity and quantum physics. Nonetheless, there is no denying that all of that was latent in the original informative theory of the heliocentric theory, and unfolded by other thinkers and mathematicians to become the basis for all those elaborations. Each advancement that this theory went through was prompted by *deductive* understanding of the informative aspects of the theory.

Psychoanalysis—in many ways—is similar in being a multilayered theory, with a little difference. The informative part of the theory was slow in gathering and every time it reached a certain level of clarity it needed to be revised (not corrected). Thus, the informative theory of psychoanalysis has never reached a point at which the leap to its final structural base was imminent. There are two issues to consider in that regard: (1) Psychoanalysis is not a natural science that has defined informational facts to be surpassed. As a human science it comprises information that could only be revised. (2) Psychoanalysis grew from being a study of some human states like psychopathology to a total theory of the individual. However, its development and the revisions it went through were reached via *inductive* thinking. As such, psychoanalysis is different from the main informative theories of the natural sciences, because it is founded on inductive thinking not on deductions like the nomothetic theories. Inductive thinking requires honing in on the right questions to ask in order to do the revising, a process that is essentially intuitive (Politzer 1928–1994).

It is difficult not to realize that the informative theory of psychoanalysis—now—has reached its limits and we need to go beyond it to its structural base. However, there is a problem in finding a direct way to do that, because the informative theory gives the impression that it was built on material. Clinical data was *usually* conceptualized in causal relationships; a characteristic of the *functional* theories of the nomothetic sciences. Analysts always puzzled about the bifurcation of clinical vs. conceptual theories, between scientific vs. hermeneutic, humanistic vs. physical, etc. Therefore, if we want to move from the informative theory to its structural foundation we have to consider those dualities to decide which structural theory we want to move to. Richards (1990) made a separation between a theory of the mind and a theory of practice, but what is important in his paper are his comments on the attitude analysts take regarding the future of those two aspects. He stated that analysts tolerate greater revisions of the psychoanalytic theory of the mind than revising the theory of therapy, *indicating more concern about the profession than what is practiced in that profession*. This point is imperative in speculating about future psychoanalysis. If we consider psychoanalysis to have two separate theories of the two separate entities then we have to find two structural bases for future psychoanalysis. But if we believe that psychoanalysis is one theory which comprises both aspects we would be taking a different approach in configuring the structural theory of psychoanalysis.

ELEMENTARY FEATURES OF STRUCTURAL THEORY

The problems those bifurcations put in the way of identifying the structural theory of psychoanalysis have a history. Prior to those new dichotomies, the debate centered on whether psychoanalysis was a theory of *intrapsychic* or of *interpersonal* issues. This debate was fundamentally flawed, because Freud's observations on the individual were on the intrapsychical dynamics and their structural impact on his interpersonal life. Thus, Freud did not consider the intrapsychical a separate entity to be studied in isolation of the totality of the psychological life of the person. In spite of the changes in the objectives of its practice that were suggested by Ferenczi, Rank, Alexander, and others a few decades before it still remained one theory. In the mid-1970s and after some analysts like G. Klein, Holt, and Wallerstein envisaged extracting from the one theory of psychoanalysis a distinctive and pure clinical theory. The separation of the clinical from the conceptual in the one theory peeked in the United States during those two decades but did not catch any fire elsewhere. This wave of "reformation" was accompanied by efforts to deduce from the theory other points of view that could change and improve the disused informative aspects. Although those attempts failed to materialize, they highlighted and forced the dichotomy of psychoanalysis as a profession and as a "general theory" of the psyche. In the meantime, the psychoanalytic organization had to deal with the aforementioned crisis in the last chapter, which uncovered possible links between the dichotomies of clinical vs. conceptual theories and analysis vs. analysts. After another half of a century of debating those issues, we now have more than one psychoanalysis, more than one clinical protocol, and more sub-organization under the auspices of the IPA. Yet, contemporary psychoanalysts do not see anything wrong with separating the practice of psychoanalysis from what is practiced. Primarily, psychoanalysis is a theory of the intra-dynamic foundation of psychical life, therefore we practice a theory of the intra-dynamics of the patient and we cannot separate theory from practice. This approach to the subject-matter of psychoanalysis emphasizes the fundamental need to work on a structural theory which explains the informative details of that subject in the same terminology we use to explain our practice.

The intrapsychic has become a common term in psychodynamic psychologies in general. We should not ignore that the intrapsychical dynamics are the psychoanalytic equivalent of *structuralism*, which pervades all the human sciences from language (Barthes 1983; Cassirer 1944; Sapir 1939; de Saussure 1912), to anthropology (Levi-Strauss 1963) passing by philosophy in its phenomenological base. The structural theories in the humanities bring out the interrelationships within the phenomenon instead of the preoccupation with the functional links between the separate entities of the phenomena. Therefore, because the intrapsychical was the initial and original proposition of psychoanalysis, it is imperative to underline the importance of this basic premise to avoid future distortion in the search of future psychoanalysis. The intrapsychical argument should be evident in any future theoretical formulation.

The structural theory of psychoanalysis is not concerned with psychical phenomena; it endeavors to highlight the originators of the psychical processes. For instance, the functional cause of transference is supressed memories in regard to some childhood experiences with a parental figure. The effect is reliving the lost memory in a repetition of the relationship with the analyst (or other characters in the patient's life). The structural basis of the transference phenomenon is the facility of the transformation of a psychical event into another psychical event. Transference in functional terms is resistance but structurally is a substitute for lost memories. The difference is major, because interpreting transference in the first explanation is conditional on its negative or positive nature (Freud 1912b) while in the second structural meaning it is a phenomenon in its own right regardless of its nature. The structural theory of psychoanalysis is founded on four conceptions that are interlinked and unite the majority of the concepts of the functional (informative) theory.

1. Affect (not feeling) is the originator of psychical phenomena. This notion is found in Freud's earliest work: the *Project* (1950a). Affect is a structural concept because it was Freud's name for the elementary reaction to satisfaction and frustration of needs. Thus, affect is the manifestation of the state of the subject at a certain condition and not a particular feeling regarding the external world. Transforming affect into feeling, emotions, mentation, and finally relationships is the originator of all that is psychical.

2. *Trieb* represents the process that differentiates between responding to external stimuli (cognitively) and the reaction to endosomatic stimuli (mental representation). The distinction between the two sources of stimulation and the two types of responses (also in the *Project*) is structurally fundamental. Sandler and Rozenblatt (1962) said: "A representation can be considered to have a more or less enduring existence as an organization or schema which is constructed out of a multitude of impressions" (132).

There are sensory organs that define the external stimulus, thus it could be identified as a cause for the response, because this process is guided by the secondary processes. The internal stimulus has to be represented in the mind and the subject would respond to the representation and not to the stimulus. The representation of the internal stimulus is dependent on the working of the primary process and its metaphoric and metonymic qualities.

3. The primary process and the secondary process are entwined in every aspect of our psychical life because no external stimulus would affect a response without activating an internal stimulus. Novey (1958) said: "Conscious perception can occur only after a physical sensory experience has been worked over in the unconscious; in this respect sensory stimuli from without are equivalent in kind to stimuli arising from within the organism. A conscious perceptual experience is bound by the principle of secondary revision (elaboration) in the waking state as well as in dreams" (79).This is exactly what happens with endosomatic stimulus which needs an external stimulus to formulate the metaphor or the metonymy that will represent it. The entwinement of the primary process and the secondary process links the external and the internal and creates

the compound of consciousness and the aconscious which permeates all our mental processes.

4. The entwinement of the primary and the secondary processes is systemically unconscious, i.e., it is not conscious or preconscious at any moment. This is a basic structural attribute of the theory of psychoanalysis (the classical theory or the Freudian doctrine), because all the details of the informative theory find a collective framework in the notion of the systemic unconscious. The concept of *Trieb* (the originator of the process of mental representation) pushed the workings of the primary process to the forefront more clearly than it was presented in the *Interpretation of Dreams*. *Trieb* is a structural conception, while the two dualities embodied in it whether it is sexuality vs. self-preservation, or life vs. death play a functional role in psychoanalysis. Its structural importance extends to creating the basic dualities of *primary vs. secondary* and *primal vs. sequel,* and several other central concepts that form the spine of the structural theory. *Trieb* made it possible to identify the processes that have original psychical origin and produce their secondary states: primary as in primary process, primary masochism, and primary narcissism. The primary lurks in the background of its corresponding secondary states all the time, and does not disappear but maintains a link with its origin in different degrees and forms. *Trieb* highlighted the other group of primal originators. The primal—like primal repression, primal fantasies, primal family, primal scene, and primal identification—eventually creates sequels that replace it and cause it to almost vanish.

Creating structural qualities of the mentioned phenomena underscores the existence of links between the poles of those dualities. Those links are first unconscious, and second are subject to evolving. Thus they become subject to proper and improper evolutions and become where we encounter health and sickness. The theory in this way is a theory of processes and not of relations. Processes pertain to the change in the psychical events and not to the changed events themselves. This feature is most obvious in the evolution of the initial sense of awareness of the other and how it leads to the secondary state of relating to another for self-interest, i.e., from primary narcissism to secondary narcissism. The most distinct characteristic of such structural theory is the place of the systemic unconscious *Ucs.* in it. It deals with the links between the primary and the secondary and between the primal and its sequel. The framework of the theory allows discovering several other connections between seemingly unrelated psychical events. It reveals, for instance, a connection between fixation and the compulsion to repeat, and between formal regression and temporal regression. The consistency of the structural theory comes from the concordance of its structural concepts and the emphasis on processes. Processes affect more than a single psychical event at the same time because they could be sharing the same structural basis. For instance, if the dream is a fulfillment of a wish and the symptom also fulfills a wish then we can conclude that they are both similarly structured. Another example: primal repression fits a concept of systemic unconscious and gives meaning to the formation of primary narcissism, which in turn becomes an originator of identification and fixation. Instead of offering cause-effect explanations as the case in the informative theory, the structural theory reveals the links between a psychical event and another if they participate in constituting an intrapsychical core. Such theory was Freud's *project-in-progress*. It did not get a final configuration because the formation of the psychical and interrelationships between its constituents needed information that could come only from other sources, and not from clinical psychoanalysis alone. This type of theory does not apprise anything important but structures our way of thinking, i.e., a theory that teaches us how to think instead of giving us thoughts. This is the type of theory that will be the basis of future psychoanalysis.

THE STRUCTURAL THEORY AND THE FORMATION OF THE ANALYST

Despite the fact that most analysts are not mindful of the structural aspect of psychoanalysis, it was inevitable for them to realize that the informative theory is one consistent theory even with all the changes and revisions it went through. From the beginnings of psychoanalysis Freud was able to read the hysterical symptoms and discover the denounced and censured wishes behind them. He was able to show that hysterical symptoms "say something about what caused them." This act was never lost or changed in all the additions, modifications, and revisions he made to the theory. In the meantime, Freud was doing the same thing with the non-clinical phenomena he studied, i.e., he was able to read in social, literary, and historical occurrences implicit and "unconscious" meanings. His findings dazzled the world and attracted to psychoanalysis some of the most talented intellectuals of the twentieth century. Freud presented to the world a unique way of thinking about the human phenomena in all its states and conditions. Clinically, analysts developed an attitude toward the act of analyzing, which for a long time was distinct and definable. It only varied lately with theoretical plurality. It is interesting to look back and examine the thinkers' and the general public's *assimilation* psychoanalytic thinking.

After centuries of theorizing about human attributes like empathy, compassion, loyalty, and other positive qualities, and at the same time the source of all human miseries, the questions of who and what is a human subject could not be found. Another problem that faced thinkers over the years was the human subject's mental health, because he was the only animal that gets mentally sick. Freud was the first to work on this latter problem. The theory opened the world's eyes to a range of human phenomena which were always considered within inflexible and predetermined frameworks like nature, morality, traditions, and unrelated issues to the subject himself. His intuition was quick to point him to the fact that there are no demarcation lines in the realm of the human subject between his many attributes and his proclivity to turn any of those attributes into a pathological condition. Thus, psychoanalysis became the answer to the myriad of questions thinkers and scientists were posing about their subject matter without an answer.

The clinical theory, especially in its early stages, was limited in the information it provided, although it was a turning point in understanding and treatment of psychopathology. It evolved to remain the leading theory in the clinical field for a century. But Freud's expansion of the boundaries of that theory was welcomed by the non-clinical intellectuals and the public in general. They were better prepared, cultured, and eager to learn about the human subject than the clinicians. They found their way to the structural foundation of psychoanalysis with clarity and eagerness, even with ease. The clinical theory (functional) is ontology of psychical contents, and is sufficient to deal with the outcome of therapy. The structural theory is ontology of the psychical processes, which is more to the liking and the proclivities of thinkers who wanted to deal with the human subject in his entirety. As mentioned before, the structural foundation of the theory had to be elicited from Freud's work on explaining the functioning of the primary process, for instance. It was inherent in his understanding of the manifest dream, in the manner he concluded the unconscious links between the preconscious and aconsciousness, from noticing that symptoms are representations of those links, and from the existence of the dynamic interactions between identification and narcissism which he expressed in the term *narcissistic-identification* (1917e), etc. It is a theory of what structures the intrapsychical nature of the subject, not what the structure of the subject is made of.[1]

However, the structural theory, after being induced from the informative theory, made non-clinicians produced a different non-clinical psychoanalysis. The literary art ventured in writing about human relations from a psychological point view with clarity and skill, and to re-evaluate some landmark works from a purely psychological point of views (*Crime and Punishment* by Dostoyevsky, *Madam Bovary* by Flaubert, etc.). The human factor has begun to take shape and occupy a prominent place in understanding human phenomena in all aspects of life. Gradually and finely the whole Western society was practicing psychoanalysis (without a license). *The most significant outcome of the permeation of psychoanalysis in everyday life was the appearance of features of a more deep-rooted theory of psychoanalysis beyond even the structural theory.* When a theory is understood and used for a while by more than its specialists it reveals—with no failing—deeper and more basic features of its potential; that is what happened with the structural theory of psychoanalysis. It revealed a way of thinking which matches the new phenomena it revealed.

I will mention first five interlinked stages in thinking structurally in psychoanalysis to show the influence of that theory on the analyst's mind. Those stages were intertwined with the natural way of thinking of the non-clinical thinkers to the point that they did not notice their impact on their new understanding of the human subject. Psychoanalysis became a comprehensive theory of the human subject. Yet clinical psychoanalysts remained reluctant to admit that non-analysts could think analytically (Arlow and Brenner 1988; Bornstein 2001; Cooper 1990; Royden and Astely 1974; Schachter 2005). It is better to begin with relaying those five stages in the clinical sphere and move to the non-clinical sphere later.

The first stage is considering the transformations that take place in the newly born to bring out his basic somato-affective nature, which will progress to become the manifestations of his nature as a human subject and his character. Whatever the attribute the analyst chooses to tackle in a person he is expected to see it within a historical dimension, and gets its developmental history. Psychoanalysts deal with the history of the psychological event as they deal with the event itself, e.g., the evolution of the intersubjective nature of that person's existence.

The second is keeping in focus the originators of any psychical manifestation of such transformations. In any theory of psychoanalysis the analyst has to account for the source of the attribute which he considers to be of paramount significance. For instance, if the analyst is addressing a type of intersubjectivity in a certain person, he has to have and to give an understanding of what generated that type of intersubjectivity, and relate it to something specific about the person.

The third stage is referring the transformations to their psychical conditions and express that in three metapsychological modalities. In one way, the requirement to be able to address the economical, dynamic, and topographical aspects of the transformation would test the analyst's understanding of what he is addressing. This point needs some clarification because metapsychology was deemed unessential for the practice of psychoanalysis. The vocabulary of metapsychology is the only way analysts could use to talk to each other about their practice with the least chance of misunderstanding. If I wanted to write about a patient I have to relate the pressures he was dealing with (economic or degree), the other factors that were interacting with that pressure (the dynamics of the material and their impact on the transference), and the links between the *Ucs.*, *Pcs.*, and *Cs.* as they influenced the process of interpretation and reconstruction. This stage of thinking is easily dismissed by analysts missing the fact that the informative theory is a theory of the psychologies of the person's attributes, thus we cannot ignore the need for metapsychology to speak about that psychology. Freud did what all psychologists do in finding the appropriate vocabulary for their psychological theories. He invented the metapsychlogies that fit his discovered psychology, as the behaviorists coined the terminology that suited the relationship between the stimuli and the behavioral response, and made it their way of communicating.

The fourth stage is postulating that what he addressed was representations of the psychical phenomena and not the phenomena itself. Representations are generated by the two main mechanisms of metonymy and metaphor. Metaphors and metonymies produce a great deal of psychological processes. Therefore, the analyst realizes that he has to read in the metaphors and metonymies the meaning of the representation. As an example, a patient developed the habit of forgetting paying his bill until he is reminded. The analyst one month forgot to give the patient his bill. After a few days the patient reminded the analyst of the bill. The patient was able to read the analyst's metaphor of forgetting the bill and a very condensed transference-counter transference situation unfolded. In other terms, the psychoanalytic way of thinking took the analyst beyond forgetting to pay or forgetting to bill and revealed unconscious exchange of mutual disrespect, i.e., it was not forgetting but disguised mutual insults. This point could shed light on the futility of the object relations and the intersubjective approach to psychoanalysis: they are merely representational material of the intrapsychical.

The fifth stage is a product of psychical life being—in essence—made of representations of the somato-affective stimulation of the mind (*Trieb*). Its theory is based on the aconscious workings of the primary process, permeating thus the whole of the psychical life of the subject and not only his attributes as a person. There is nothing outside the reach of the process of representation, and a psychoanalyst has to contend with that fact: he deals with metaphors and metonymies that express the human subject's *Modus Operandi.*

The first two stages are the main breakthroughs toward a psychology of the subject. Before the birth of psychoanalysis, the natural response to a person's behavior was to name it, judge it, and give it a meaning derived from a certain background like social, moral, religious, etc. Psychoanalysis changed that attitude in Western and Westernized societies. Understanding human behavior has become the work of specialists and is always done in reference to the person himself. It has become common understanding that the present of the individual is shaped by his past. We resort to knowing, deducing, or applying the culture of "the psychology of the person" as our means to understanding human nature. Looking for and making links between the person's childhood and his present state of mind is routine work for psychoanalysts and even the dynamically affected theorists. However, the work of psychoanalysis is not always done with the concept of the subject in mind, because most analysts are still either dealing with "individuals" or do not make a distinction between the individual and the human subject. A clinical example could help in making that distinction between the subject and the individual who are the same person.

One of my supervisors was a second generation psychoanalyst, analyzed by M. Klein, and was a "real" Kleinian. I was reporting to him on a patient who "suffered" from feeling that his mother is always there in everything he does witnessing and judging what he does (she died few years before he started his analysis). My supervisor did not mention anything about introjecting the mother or used any other Kleinian jargon. He asked where his mother would be while she was watching him. I asked the patient that question, which at first baffled him, but after thinking for while he said she is always behind him (not seeing her face). I immediately thought of transference and that I am behind him on the couch (brilliant transference insight). I got no response from the patient or my supervisor either. The supervisor directed my attention to the patient's phantasy of his mother watching him, and asked if she is the one imposing herself on him, or he is who calls her to be watching. When I examined this point with the patient he came up with preconscious memories that surprised him as much as they did me. They were very pertinent to few other points relating to his Oedipus position. His phantasy said more things about being still living his childhood relationship with his mother: *It said more about the state of his identity than what the psychoanalytic situation meant to him.* The analytic situation pertains to the limited dynamics of the "patient" but his identity pertains to the human subject in him.

The next two stages are about the best vocabulary to use in talking about the human subject who is in treatment, and not about the individual on the couch. Psychoanalysis has the vocabulary which relates the intrapsychic dynamics of the person to him as a patient. The patient lives through representations of himself and seldom does he talk about himself directly. His representations do the talking even to himself. This is one of the most ingenious discoveries by Freud: the gap between the speaking *I* and the spoken about *me*. This distinction is implicit in everything psychoanalysis does; however, it is either completely missed by the psychoanalyst, or expressed vaguely under other topics like narcissism or the difference between the subject and the Ego. Lacan said (1977): "[Freud] wrote *Das Ich Und Das Es* in order to maintain this fundamental distinction between the true subject of the unconscious and the ego as constituted by a series of alienations" (128). Therefore, it could be said that ego psychology missed its target and created instead a distraction from the real issue.

Psychoanalysis imparts a basic attitude in dealing with humans in light of the first four aforementioned stages.[2] The fifth stage is the central one in the structural theory of psychoanalysis. The subject is alienated in representations, and the representations permeate all his psychical life, therefore where could we find the true *subject of the unconscious* as Lacan called him? There is no subject of consciousness to have a subject of the unconscious. What we have is a subject who appears as an object of consciousness and occupies a place in it, either as an authentic representation of himself or a false representation. He is never totally himself and he is always partially authentic in presenting himself. The subject of the unconscious is the same subject of consciousness with one distinction: the authenticity of his representations. There is a basic difference between someone in pain talking and someone talking about his pain. The former's speech will be authentic and revealing the psychological pain by choosing painful things to talk about. The latter would be informing or reporting about himself as someone suffering from psychological pain but almost as he would report about someone else. Furthermore, once a person becomes conscious of his psychological state he gets alienated in his consciousness of himself; he becomes aware of his awareness and loses the authenticity of reporting.

The case mentioned above allowed going beyond the meaning of the "symptom" (the reported suffering), which was weaved in the phantasy of the watching mother. Leaving the symptom aside and talking about whose wish it was for the mother to exist in the patient's life facilitated more associations about the Oedipus situation in the family. The patient realized that he was calling his mother to mind for her to witness what he was doing. He then talked about his father's womanizing escapades and his mother taking it masochistically and acquiescing to his father's light-hearted attitude toward his role in the family. He grew up to be very unlike his father. At first I was distracted by the typical psychoanalytic theoretical explanations of the "content" of the material and ignored that the patient structured *his* life situation on the blue print of the Oedipal model of his family. His associations showed that he did with himself what he would have wished his mother to do with the father. Still captivated by the traditional psychoanalytic theory, I thought that his phantasy was an expression of his need for his mother's presence to stop him from doing what his father used to do. This is a common attitude candidates take from their patients: they deal with them as generic patients who demonstrate the typical psychoanalytic postulates. Refraining from giving a classical interpretation was rewarded by the patient accepting that he was "saying" to his mother: "see I am better than father." The patient's phantasy proved to be his subjective structuring of the Oedipal triangulation; something that goes with the conception of the Oedipus but in its subjective and personal version. His intrapsychical structure was encapsulated in his father's identity. His mother was not introjected to form a superego, or that he was fixated on a pregenital phase of development, etc.; he was transferring the analytic situation on a childhood position. The patient's Oedipal triangulation was structured in such a manner that it needed to be explored and examined by the patient and not by him.

In this supervisory experience (and several others with the same supervisor) I learned two things and discovered a third on my own much later.

(1) The patient is not a *generic* person who is only different from others because to his personal psychopathology. Patients are unique human subjects, and in applying psychoanalysis in their treatment we are likely to discover what the symptom means to the patient. But, if we go beyond analyzing symptoms of psychopathology, the picture changes and our work takes a different color. Going beyond the symptom in search of the originators of the individual's life situation would reveal that the symptom is only one aspect of the *representation of a personal drama*. In this patient the symptom of his mother haunting him was only an aspect of a familial drama that created that symptom. Symptoms are not the pathology of the individual but they only impart a determining situation that produced that particular subject. In fact, as scarce as the clinical material in Freud's text was, it was always about human subjects who were shaped by life experiences, not by pathological events that formulated their neuroses, as analysts prefer to think. My supervisor's shift from the expected and analytically known to the unexpected about the connotation of the phantasy was remarkable (the patient was the one who wanted his mother around). It showed me that each psychoanalytic experience is very much similar to the discovery of psychoanalysis itself. If we accept that Freud's journey in psychoanalysis was a trip toward locating the human subject in the individual, and that he did it without a map to guide him or a blueprint of what to be looking for, then the proper way to do psychoanalysis should be exactly like Freud's journey; no map or blueprint in doing psychoanalysis or relying on the informative aspect of the theory. Politzer formulated this feature in the Freudian theory by saying:

> Let us open any of Freud's writings: the report is always based on individual facts, and what is essential is that the individual character, far from disappearing in the course of the explanation [the informative aspect], always remains the main point . . . the study of neurosis with Freud is not . . . the study of the *neuroses in themselves*, in these marvelous nosological entities that the individuals incarnate and for the study of which this incarnation has no importance, but on the contrary, each neurosis is like an individual act that we must explain as being individual. It is natural that in these conditions we end with the constitution of particular facts from which the generalization becomes possible, but one which, once made becomes applicable to a multitude of particular cases, putting psychoanalysis in possession of a true knowledge. (1994/1928, 48–49)

Politzer, a philosopher, made the distinction between individual information and the truth about the human subject eleven years before

Freud's death, while analysts are still reluctant to consider the importance of making that distinction.

(2) Discovering the subject is not only the main objective of analysis; it is also the only objective the patient has in mind coming to psychoanalysis. The patient suffers from misidentifying his original need and being alienated in his personality and losing his subjectivity. This conception differs from treating a patient as an abnormal person who could be restored to normality, which is an impression analysts convey to their patient in subtle ways. For instance, a religious patient was having a very difficult time giving up what her mother had identified her as in her childhood (my perfect daughter). She discovered in herself a different, adult identity that she wanted to assume to replace the obsessive childhood one. She was praying—in total devotion and sincerity—for a miracle that would change her to that mature person. I said once: "God might listen to your prayers one day and the next day you wake up to be that different person." She panicked and explained her anxiety by stating that she would not know who she is. Fundamentally, the patient wanted to achieve a true subjectivity, which she precociously knows, but was unable to assume it due to the anxiety of the neurotic (childish) "person" who she was.

(3) I learned on my own after many years that the transformation of the somato-affective origins of the psychical comes in the patients' associations in the form of phantasies, i.e., phantasies are transformations of endosomatic stimulations. Better, phantasies are a stage in the process of transforming the endosomatic state into psychical representations. They are also the first step in the transformation of the endosomatic into something psychical like symptoms, relationships, or even linguistic patterns. Isaacs (1948) showed in an inspiring way the link between the metaphors the patient uses and his fantasies. Unfortunately there was no follow up on this point in a guided way. Hence, the Kleinian were fascinated from the beginning by fantasies, and built the major part of the theory of the *interpersonal* around that, because phantasies to them were the closest they were able to get to the intrapsychic.

Reisner averred that (1999) "the single stumbling block in contemporary use of Freud's contribution stems from the belief that psychoanalysis is a specific interpretation of behaviors and motivations, rather than a way of thinking about and organizing psychological processes" (1039). It would help to identify the features of analytic thinking. The aforementioned five stages in the structural way of thinking in psychoanalysis are the foundation of a conception of the human subject. They are Freud's *implicit* understanding of the manner which leads to the structuring of the human subject. The human subject—with maturity—develops the ability to control responding to stimuli and delays his reaction thus creating an intermediate phase between them. In that intermediate phase the nature the person is constituted and becomes a permanent infrastructure through which the rest of the person's reactions will be determined. Humans do not eat when their energy is sapped (endosomatic state), but they feel hungry first and hunger drives them to eat. As analysts we know the strange and many feelings that hunger could generate in a person, ranging from temper to creative mental products. The human subject is the only primate who reacts to his somatic needs since his birth, by generating representations of himself to himself as a first step toward acting upon them. Those representations are the social medium that humans use in their interaction (when that process fails and the animal in us breaks through our human quality).

THE FORMATION OF THE ANALYSTS AND THE PSYCHOLOGY OF THE SUBJECT

Psychoanalysis is not limited to an informative theory about the dynamics of the individual, whether in sickness or in health; it reached a level of sophistication to generate a structural theory of the psychical phenomena in its rich permutations. The structural theory of psychoanalysis exposed a subtle difference between the individual as the common denotation of a person and the human subject as an entity that encompasses the individual. The individual is not the human subject, though the subject is the individual. The individual has a *persona*[3] that objectifies him but does not represent his subjectivity. The familiar theory of psychoanalysis, and all the other informative theories that claim to be psychoanalytical, is about the individual as an object. It talks about aspects, elements, attributes, and entities that could be identified in that individual, or talks about the object's mental, emotional, ego strength conditions, "his" defense mechanisms, object-relations, and analyzability. The patient or the individual who enters our office has more to him as a human subject than what he thinks and what he will reveal to us. An obsessive-compulsive patient who is precariously balancing his sadistic tendencies and his paternal love could also be a reliable friend, music lover, or artist.

It is better to explain this distinction by using Freud's unsuccessful effort and attempts at formulating a final statement about his discoveries. Before 1905, Freud thought that he has an aetiological theory of psychoneuroses based on the repression of the sexual urge, which is what makes the subject gets sick. But he quickly realized that the sexual aspect in the neuroses is not the cause but the effect of infantile sexual experiences that are particular to each single neurotic person. After making that deduction he examined the various features of psychical life (review his work between 1907–1914). During that period, the individual took a back seat to give his place to the processes that create those features. He then turned the theory upside down: psychoneuroses is not caused by sexual frustration but is created by infantile experiences that could also be of a sexual nature. Between 1914 and 1920, Freud discovered most of the psychical structures of the human subject, but stopped short of articulating a new theory of psychoanalysis; the structural theory. He could not abandon his aspiration to build his legacy on a final informative theory of psychoneuroses. He tried that in *The Ego and the Id* (1923b), but once again he could not canonize it as the official and final theory of psychoanalysis. *Inhibitions, Symptoms, and Anxiety* (1926d) was a good example of recognizing that the legend of psychoanalysis is going to be a theory of the subject and not of the psychoneurosis. In that work, Freud reverses his old theory of anxiety: instead of anxiety attacking the human subject because of repression, the human subject responds to his psychical condition with anxiety and forms his subjective way of dealing with it, which sometimes takes the form of symptoms.

The interesting part in that evolution is discovering the processes which constitute the subject and fit exactly in his old and persistent dictum: *understanding the normal is the way to understanding the pathological.* This implicit, or should we say formative, approaches to understanding the individual goes beyond a difference between the human subject and the individual who represents him; it explains very well the changes that occurred over the years to the population of patients. Freud had made strides in discovering what constitutes the human condition although he was fixated on his early successful breakthroughs in the field of hysteria and the psychoneuroses of that time. If psychoneurosis is a disease, sickness, or malady then it should have stayed the same since its onset in the human race (the flu is the same with some mutations in the virus). But since psychoneurosis is one of several human conditions it is natural to expect changes in the psychoneuroses over the years, as the human subject undergoes changes caused by the adjustments he introduces to his circumstances. We seldom see in our practices nowadays a case of hysterical paralysis, but we see cases of anorexia nervosa, or myalgia. What makes the neurotic picture changes over the years? The answer is the human subject, because he structures his neuroses. Future psychoanalysis has to deal with the human condition: its structure sometimes becomes symptomatic.

The structural theory—even if the analyst is not fully cognizant of its influence—shapes his mind. An experienced supervising-training analyst knows well that he cannot make an analyst out of a candidate by merely reviewing with him the week's material of his patient's sessions, guiding him toward some unconscious aspects in the material that he did not notice, the way an interpretation is better formulated to allow other material to remerge, or a difference between a good construction and a bad one. Those are details in a complex set-up of patient-candidate and candidate-supervisor. Supervisors do not train candidates to become analysts; they discover the analysts in some of them. A good faculty member in the institute knows that he cannot teach psychoanalysis; he can only *show the candidates how to read* the literature to benefit from the writings of others (Freud in particular). To demonstrate what I am saying I will give two examples from Freud's text, which show two typically informative statements that could mean nothing if the structural theory has not prepared the analyst's mind to understand. In *The Ego and the Id* (1923b) Freud says: "By setting up this ego ideal, the ego has mastered the Oedipus complex and at the same time placed itself in subjection to the id" (36). This sentence speaks of things that we should recognize if they existed. But what could we do if they are not in a form to identify (id is not a psychical entity but a name given to urges and motives supposed to exist but are not conscious to identify). The analyst who has assimilated the perspective of the transformation of the somato-affective in psychical manifestation would know that Freud was talking about the subject's family triangulation and his identification with the father to regulate his passions and attachments to the mother. In *Analysis Terminable and Interminable* (1937c) Freud gave three conditions that we are supposed to meet in the process of termination: the strength of the trauma, the deformation of the ego, and the strength of the *Trieben*. This piece of information is useless if we do not know what constitutes the strength of a trauma or of the *Trieben*, which we actually have no means to know. The deformation of the ego is also something that is impossible to identify in a manner that will guide us through termination. Analysts who did not assimilate the structural aspect of psychoanalysis would find the information in this statement unfathomable. Most likely the analyst would put the blame on metapsychology, which is merely a vocabulary for the psychology of affect and its transformations. Analysts who integrated the structural aspect of the theory in their approach would understand that abstract sentence about termination as a request to assess the strength of the compulsion to repeat, the ability of the person to respond to the circumstance and not to his own self-concept, and the flexibility in reading more in external givens.

A theory of that nature is formative because it does not give any information but only direction to understanding the material differently. Instead of understanding the person through his attributes it forces understanding the human subject through the processes that form him, thus learning more about the person who is personalizing him. The process of understanding the human subject obliges the analyst to encounter several lacking features in the picture, and has to induce them from the material offered, which could disguise well those lacks. A patient who is regularly or irregularly late or mostly silent in the sessions presents a lack, e.g., something that should be there but is missing. There is no way to teach anyone how to look for that lack; this is what distinguishes a good analyst from a not-so-good one. *If there are differences between analysts it would not be in knowing the literature better or learning more from it, but it will be in recognizing in their practice what could explain what they read.*

THE NEED FOR THE STRUCTURAL THEORY IN FUTURE PSYCHOANALYSIS

The diagnostic categories and the symptomatology of the new nosologies force us to consider the relevance of the informative theory of psychoanalysis from a different angle. Hysteria and the obsessive-compulsive neurosis are very rare to encounter in current clinical practice. It is more common now to see patients diagnosed with narcissistic conditions, or character disorders mainly because of difficulties in their interpersonal relationships, or unhappiness with their own comportment. However, it is not definite that the old psychopathologies have disappeared, which would be—by itself—the end of the informative theory of psychoanalysis. It is possible that we are still dealing with the old diagnostic entities with different symptomatologies and not with totally different psychopathologies. For a few decades in the last century psychoanalysts did a good job of using the old model of psychopathology to widen the understanding of the commonplace psychopathological conditions. They were also able to use the structural theory, particularly in the conception of narcissism, in eliciting new conditions that were previously considered out of the reach of psychoanalysis.[4] Freud informative theory about psychopathological dynamics did not cover the new pathologies, nevertheless analysts continued "unconsciously" using the terminology of that theory in dealing with those cases. They were not fully aware that they learned from psychoanalysis a parallel theory (the structural theory) that preserved the basic premise of the psychodynamics of the intrapsychic regardless of the nosological name given to a particular psychopathology.[5]

The cultural and social changes that were—to a great extent—instigated by psychoanalysis changed the manifestations of the person, but did not change the nature of the human subject. In Freud's time the rise of the bourgeois class strove to control women's aspirations (the budding future of a social revolution), and separate men's domination from their sexual performance. The result was the pervasiveness of the female hysterical personality with symptoms revealing women's sexual frustrations. Men were equally sexually inept but did not display similar symptoms women, probably to keep their domination over them. It was natural that psychical problems changed in nature after the bourgeois's class lost its "class," and with the sexual revolution of the 1960s. Added to that was the shrinking of the extended family and the appearance of the nuclear family instead, as the more common social unit, limiting the previous ease and range of displacements. The fact of the matter is that after the active role women played in World War II real social changes materialized. There was gradual disappearance of the familiar diagnoses of hysteria and obsessive-compulsive neuroses, which were replaced with the diagnoses of disorders like "schizoid personality disorder," "borderline personality disorder," "narcissistic personality disorder," "depressive disorders," and now the "interpersonal disorders." A good question should be asked here: Could it be that the traditional psychoneuroses have found social solutions, or are they still there but called disorders instead? It is likely that *the dissemination of psychoanalytic thinking in the society and the gradual assimilation of the structural theory of the psychoanalytic circles led to recognizing the human subject as he was never noticed before.* The human subject is an individual who absorbed the psychoanalytic vocabulary and is directly using it in expressing his discomforts. Instead of a woman fainting in a crowded place to stop sexual harassment as she did before, she would now belligerently accuse the males around her of harassment, and possibly her behavior is called sometimes a "disorder." It is common that the same psychoanalytic insights are active everywhere. A Supreme Court judge would spontaneously think that his son's drug problems must be due to his conflicts with his mother, while his driver knows that his son's aspirations to study law is because of admiring the man whom his father drives to work every day.

Social assimilation of the psychoanalytic way of thinking has changed the attitude of the patients toward psychological help. In Freud's time, it was rare for someone to consider himself in need for psychological help if he did not have obvious symptoms, and mostly symptoms that have physical manifestations. Patients, at that time, had to have psychological sickness to go for treatment. Nowadays, people are more aware of their psychological conditions and do not seek treatment because of being psychologically sick. I have a personal experience to demonstrate that change. Fifty years ago, when I started to practice in Egypt, patients came complaining of symptoms like I have a fear of men, or I have a need to prove myself. Seldom did a patient say I am unable to establish a relationship with men, or I am always expecting humiliation from others. Those patients could not understand how laying on a couch and free associating would get them rid of their symptoms. After immigrating to Canada and getting further training, I met the sophisticated patient who knew that he was sick without having symptoms. Thirty-five years later I went back to Egypt for a few years and practiced there. I had patients of the first type whom I referred to psychiatrist and who did well on anxiolytics and anti-depressants. But, there were new kinds of patients who needed psychoanalysis and asked for it in its classical form. Once psychoanalysis became available there was a big demand for it. Patients were clear about what they were seeking: to be treated and not to get treatment for their symptoms. The difference is that symptoms to the individual are the sickness that wants to get rid of, but the human subject knows that symptoms are the result of being sick and needing to be treated. The assimilation of the psychoanalytic way of thinking is a formative process that differentiates between the analyst and non-analyst on the one hand,

and between the analytic patient and non-analytic patient on the other hand.

Most patients in the West, and we can also assume a growing number in the East are aware of the difference. I am also sure that psychotherapists in the West know that the aim of therapy is not to treat symptoms anymore but to change the person. Yet there is a problem with the aspiration of most psychotherapies. They derive their informative theories from the traditional psychoanalytic tradition; nevertheless they do not offer a definable conception of what their therapeutic objectives are. It is the same within the contemporary psychoanalytic schools; they are—more or less—informative psychoanalyses without a clear structural basis for their concepts. Current clinical psychoanalysis is missing two of the most distinct and important features of its classical form. First is the modality of psychosexual development and its corresponding system of diagnosis. Freud envisaged a model of psychological development based on the natural vital sequence of the endogenous needs and their corresponding bodily organs. He specifically named them: oral, anal, and phallic. Each of those organs is considered erogenic (sexualized) because their physiological nature is associated with and provides sensual pleasure, which becomes part of sexual life in maturity. When a vital function is activated—and the infant is going through its pressure on his mind—the organ that serves that function would influence the production of representations of that endosomatic stimulus. It also deals with the possible conflicts it generates and the resolutions of those conflicts, builds its specific intrapsychical structure, and the specific patterns of success or failure. Those specific patterns consolidate the intrapsychic structure of that erogenic zone which eventually becomes the interrelationship pattern of that human subject. Freud put the need for nourishment as the most vital immediately after birth. Controlling bowel movement was the second most vital because it coincides with the onset of socialization and early independence. With less physical dependency on the mother and the widening of the social scope, sexual identification becomes the third stage in that development. A fourth stage follows, which is not associated with any part of the body but temporarily integrates the previous experiences and keeps them latent until puberty comes to reactivate them. The human subject thus is borne along with the idiosyncrasies of the individual who will personify him later in life. Erickson (1952) expressed this notion by eliciting character formation pertaining to each of those stages in this model of development, e.g., the resolution of the demand of each stage of development forms its corresponding intrapsychic structure that is expressed in a personal character.

Parallel to the stages of development Freud and his disciples (Abraham in particular) furnish a foundation for psychodynamic explanations of psychopathology related to that model of development. They even tried to correlate certain neuroses with each stage of development (Fliess

1956). Although it was a little stretched ambition, it is not something to sneer at. The pioneers of psychoanalysis were professional enough to know that in order to embark on a therapeutic act the analyst should start with a diagnosis—an elementary idea of what he would be dealing with. Second, they knew that nosology in their time did not have a place for the discoveries of psychodynamic. Therefore, they tried something in between based on the nosology of their time, particularly in regard to the psychoneuroses. They speculated about the appropriate psychodynamics which could produce those symptomologies (for instance, anal problems would generate the obsessions). The attempt seemed to have been workable then, but it is not so now after the diagnostic categories have changed. Recent attempt at having a new system (Psychodynamic Diagnostic Manual 2008) was rudderless because of the absence of a clearly defined theory of psychoanalysis and the absence of a developmental modality. If we had sort of a unified theory of psychoanalysis we could have made the proper classification that explains the psychopathology.

Current psychoanalysis is still dealing with the same processes that built the intrapsychical structures and their possible failures, because nothing has changed the main model of psychosexual development. However, those same failures create psychoneuroses that have different symptomatologies. An example, which is very common in current practices, is the young successful professional who has healthy business relationships but is inhibited, unsuccessful in his social life, limited in his interests, and incapable of enjoying anything outside the workplace. There is no specific diagnosis to give to this picture. After a period of psychoanalysis the patient would prove to be a compulsive person without any obsessive-compulsive symptoms. Whatever our theoretical orientation, we commonly deal with early developmental problems that persist to create the existing condition of the patient. Therefore, it is only natural and essential that we need to have a developmental modality which guides our diagnosis and our therapeutic endeavors.

The second thing missing in today's psychoanalysis is equally crucial. From the beginning, and maybe until now, the classical theory of psychotherapy adopted the attitude that the clinical analyst aims at curing the patient. In the early years, Breuer and Freud believed that under hypnosis, they could remove repression, which causes the symptoms; therefore they could cure the hysterical neurosis. In spite of the changes that were made to psychoanalysis, the view that it is an act of curing patients was so much enriched that it is still its indelible epithet. It started with the idea of releasing the repressed, moved to weakening the defenses, interpreting transference resistance, strengthening the ego, treating early harmful introjections, etc. Those conceptions fit the notion that psychoanalysis is a profession and the psychoanalyst is a paid professional whose job is to cure patients. Nonetheless, as early as 1926, Freud tackled the terminabilty and the interminabilty of analyses (in an article of a heavy metaphorical flavor) and concluded that we cannot do much about two fundamental barriers to a final cure: castration anxiety in men and penis-envy in women. Figuratively speaking, psychoanalysis was not anymore a curative act, and no analyst who might have believed in Freud's conclusion could have said—with a straight face—that he really cured a patient in spite of those two rock-bottom resistances, or crossed those two barriers.

Analysts in the beginning of the 1950s implicitly acknowledged that psychoanalysis does not cure. They shifted the emphasis of incurability from analysis to the patient: Is the patient analyzable? Analysts got into discussing the analyzable diagnoses and excluded several as unsuitable for analysis (Knap et al. 1960; Bellak and Meyers 1975). Yet, some like Bellak et al. (1969–1970) wrote about using psychoanalysis with psychotic patients. When those attempts still failed to pinpoint the reason psychoanalysis—in spite of its neat theory—did not cure all patients, they tried to outline the characteristics of the patients who could benefit from psychoanalysis. They went into, more-or-less, speculative debates regarding the patient ego's capacity to ally itself with the analyst, his suitability for insight oriented psychotherapy, etc. (Firestein 2001). In France, there was some interesting work on auto-analysis (self-analysis) which should continue after termination (Anzieu 1959; Flournoy 1981). Apparently those efforts failed in dealing with Freud's pessimism of cure. Therefore analysts in the 1970s went back to the concept of termination itself. It became clear that there is no termination of any psychoanalysis, which explicitly means that psychoanalysis is not an act of curing a sickness or restoring a state of health (normality). Cure was replaced with terms like improvement, gaining insight, and even just mutual agreement on termination. Caring implies the existence of scaled states of sickness and health.

The informative theory of psychoanalysis over the years and until the 1970s revealed its limitations and usefulness as a final formulation of the Freudian theory. Nevertheless, the Freudian theory maintained its status as an irreplaceable doctrine, despite many aforementioned odds. However, it promised a structural foundation that is more fundamental and encompassing. The five stages of thinking mentioned above maintained the reliability of a theory regardless of the kind of thinking it was about, e.g., clinical or non-clinical. The structural theory provided a way of thinking that is formative of the psychoanalytic mind. The psychoanalytic mind remained the source of the novelty which kept the theory surviving for over a century, and in all likelihood will continue until we find an equivalent to replace it.

NOTES

1. Lacan's major contribution to psychoanalysis is metpsychoanalytic reformulations of Freud's structural theory, although he and his followers argue that it is psychoanalysis.

2. With little speculation we can envisage the difference in understanding patients if those aspects of transformation and several others regarding the human subject are clarified to us by child psychologists, thinkers, and professionals in those fields of knowledge. Future psychoanalysis will derive a substantial part of its new theory from being part of a wide circle of sciences and thought. Clinical psychoanalysis will not be an isolated professional endeavor without convincing theory or therapeutic outcome; it will be an important part of a host of human sciences that are dedicated to the study of the subject.

3. Persona is the mask actors in the ancient theater of Greece used to personify the character they were playing: Jupiter, Athena, an ordinary citizen, etc. The term was used later as one of three classes of pronouns and as a synonym of the individual in his bodily state. However, a person is what the individual represents to others as a presence.

4. When Freud was still thinking in terms of the libido theory he made a sweeping distinction between two kinds of psychopathologies: transference neuroses and narcissistic neuroses (1914c). The distinction was based on the limited libidinal investment in external objects in narcissistic people to allow transference to develop.

5. The contemporary theories of psychoanalysis that adopt the interpersonal approach to psychopathology have no modality of their own. Therefore, when they speak of psychopathology they have no option but to use the language of intrapsychical psychodynamics.

FOUR

Three Structural Conceptions of Psychoanalysis

In the previous chapters I underlined a distinction between the informative theory and the structural theory of psychoanalysis, stating that the informative theory comprises concepts derived from observations, some clinical and some technical. Those concepts were subject to changes and revisions depending on the changes or advancement in the observations. The structural theory, on the other hand, is a theory of main propositions that are based on grasping the abstract value of the concepts of the informative theory and establishing their interrelationships. Their abstract format is stable and institutes core viewpoints of the human subject. The first proposition stipulates that the human subject deals cognitively with the external world and psychologically with the world of the endosomatic activities. The second proposition underscores the bifurcated mind of the subject, which has no means to differentiate between the external and the internal worlds to respond to each separately. The five stages of thinking in the context of those two propositions indicate and point to the need to move on to a new and different psychoanalysis; a psychoanalysis of the subject and not the generic individual. In light of the structural theory of psychoanalysis we can see that psychoanalysis is neither a theoretical entity in its own right (natural science), nor a profession based on some technical methods in using its informative theory, nor clearly part of the idiographic group of sciences. The advancement in our way of thinking, due to the impact of the structural theory, guided the criticism of psychoanalysis as a whole and not of certain aspects of it, i.e., disillusionment of the whole informative theory. However, the evident contemporary uselessness of the informative theory should not distract from an inherent issue in the problem. The problem is not in psychoanalysis per se, but in the subject matter of psychoanalysis. In other words, classical psychoanalysis was satisfactory when it was dealing with the psychology of the individual, but we reached the limits of that psychology, and we came to recognize that the theory has a structural base which surpasses the psychology of the individual. Its structural basis is a way of thinking which leads us to change the subject matter of psychoanalysis, as the theory of evolution when it reached the limits of the idea of survival of the fittest had to move and moved to the study mutation.

The bifurcation of mental activity and the mind's inability to distinguish between cognitive and psychological responses corroborates that any human phenomenon is a manifestation of an activity that involves all three mental states of *Cs.*, *Pcs.*, and *Ucs.* The mind's response to a stimulus begins with no differentiation of what state of mind is best for it. In the best conditions it will give priority to the best state of mind to dealing with it. However, it is only reasonable to anticipate many unexpected things to happen in that process which could be responsible for creating psychical and cognitive confusions. We should also expect that whatever the outcome of the process, it will never be purely psychological or cognitive; it will be a mixture of both in different degrees. Accepting and assimilating this main characteristic of psychoanalysis would impact the analyst's mind and influence his way of thinking. It would have a formative influence on his approach to both the theory and the way he listens to the patient's material.

The structural theory has the road marks for the psychoanalytic way of thinking, which is independent of the material or the content of the process of thinking. Clinically speaking, psychoanalytic thinking would set the analyst's mind to shift spontaneously from listening to a patient reporting an event or a memory to a surreptitious usage of an unexpected metaphor while imparting his experience. The analyst's psychoanalytic mind hones on the new representation and finds it interlinked with other material that was relayed sessions before. The psychoanalytic mind reworks those interlinks and forms an interpretation or reconstruction accordingly. The new unexpected metaphoric forms are *always* the nucleus of more than one of the structural propositions of psychoanalysis because the assimilation of the structural theory and its propositions changes the analyst's way of thinking. The interconnectedness of the main conceptions of the structural theory furnishes the background and the nature of psychoanalytic thinking.

The psychoanalytic way of thinking will always carry features of the personal thinking processes of the analyst. The difference between analysts is what they would structure of the psychoanalytic material, yet structuring itself will bring them back close to where they all started. An analyst might put effort in interpreting a dream in order to explore the patient's way of free associating about it revealing the working of the primary process. Another analyst might give more attention to dreaming that dream at that particular stage in the analysis as means of revealing an aspect in the transference. Both analysts will come close to each other's objectives by structuring the dream within the process of psychoanalysis, instead of being distracted by the dream as a bearer of unconscious information. I am going to present three structural propositions that—in my own way of thinking—could be useful in showing the interconnections of some main conceptions in the informative theory.

TRIEB, REPRESENTATION, AND THE PRIMARY

Trieb is the "condition" of the endosomatic in the human subject, while instinct is that same condition in the rest of the animal kingdom. The term used to state that the origin of psychical life is affect, with the least controversy. Affect[1] is the first and the basic reaction to the endosomatic pressure on the mind. It is the beginning of a chain of transformations which gives the endosomatic pressure its representation. The first transformation becomes the prototype of the ensuing transformations. It becomes an origin in its own right and keeps generating representations. It only ceases changing when it informs a metaphor. Psychical life is born that way. *Trieb*, or the act of transforming the somatic into mental activity, is *Ucs.* and remains unconscious, but keeps generating representations and only ceases when the primary process settles on a fixed representation. For example, the pain effect of narcissistic injury in the phallic phase of development generates a chain of representations of humiliation until the primary process—in its unconscious nature—makes shyness the perpetual response to any competitive situation and the metaphor of castration.

Affect is used to indicate two states: pleasure or pain. Primary repression, which creates a cleavage between consciousness and unconsciousness, separates affect as sensation of pleasure from pain as the antithesis of pleasure. It also separates affect from its ideation (Freud 1894a; 1896b), and eventually separates inner (the representation) from the outer (the object of the representation). The sensation of pleasure after the baby finishes his meal on the breast becomes the next thing to be represented. The sensation of satiation and fullness is gradually distanced from its original endosomatic source, and gets ideational representations associated with the mother as the source of pleasure. Thus, the physical need for nourishment instigates an oral psychical life. The emergence of psychological life out of the oral transformations progresses and evolves to become a dynamic field of progression and regression, showing and validating the vicissitudes of the *Trieb*. In an enigmatic way the pleasure of satiation is represented by a sensation of fullness while of the pain of hunger finds its representation in emptiness. The verbal expressions of fullness an emptiness seem to replace the sensations as early as when the infant learn the words. One of the classical examples of that transformation was intuitively perceived by Freud in his grandchild's game of *Fort* (gone*)* *Da* (here) (Freud 1920g). Psychoanalysts—and only the ones who adhere to the classical modality of psychosexual development—discover in the speech of some patients the metaphors of fullness and the metonymies of emptiness associated with oral phantasies. The enigma is the transformation of a bodily sensation into a mental representation, with both the original affective accompaniments and the verbal metaphors. *Future psychoanalysis would be able to properly articulate that enigma and poste it for child psychologist, linguists, and neurologists, seeking their thoughts and findings about it.*

In *Studies on Hysteria,* Breuer and Freud (1895d) summarized their main discovery saying: "We found, to our great surprise, that each individual hysterical symptom immediately and permanently disappeared when we had succeeded in bringing clearly to light the memory of the event by which it was provoked and in arousing its accompanying effect. . . . Recollection without affect almost invariably produced no results" (6). In terms of a theory of pathology based on forgetting (repression) and recall (catharsis), the affective component of the repressed was considered central in the process of cure. However, it is clear from this statement and from the history of the psychoanalytic movement that what they meant was the *emotional* component of the repressed event and not affect in its raw elementary condition. Freud very perceptively noticed, even that early in the history of psychoanalysis, that cure does not happen when the strangulated feeling was abreacted or remembered under hypnosis, but when the patient becomes aware of it and could express it in his language or realizes that his symptom *says* something. When he reached that point, the phase of hypnotic therapy ended. It is important to emphasize that Freud abandoned exploring the repressed feeling as such very early in his discoveries because he recognized that the repressed is more than what is just in the sphere of feelings and emotions.

Without recognizing this beginning of psychoanalysis, the rest of the theory would become a set of disconnected concepts loosely related and each could be judged separately and on its own merits. This is the nature of informative theories. However, if we start from the conception of *Trieb* and its vicissitudes, psychoanalysis will be seen as one integral theoretical structure from its inception until where Freud left it; it was only evolving all that time. His consistent belief in the arbitrary relationship between the manifest and the latent, the object and the aim of the *Trieb,* the primary process and the secondary process, the bound and unbound energy, etc., attests to never abandoning the original proposition of affect as the originator of psychical life, even though it remained in the background for all his upcoming discoveries. The inevitability that affect acquires an adjectival quality did not lure Freud away from two codependent factors in a psychology of affect: (1) Affect is expressed and manifested in the intensity of the psychical phenomenon, an intensity that could undergo different vicissitudes, e.g., unbound energy. (2) For affect to become material of conscious quality it has to get bound to something in the ideational system, i.e., become a representation (metaphor or metonymy) where it gets a qualitative meaning (thus becomes a feeling, idea, fantasy, etc.).

Freud seems to have grasped the first factor and said clearly that there is no such thing as unconscious affects (1915c; 1923b). The term *un*-conscious denotes turning something that was originally conscious into unconsciousness, i.e., undoing consciousness. Affect originates in the *Triebhaft* sphere or the body, thus it remains an attribute of the *Ucs.* (Green 1999, 289–90). Green puts it well when he says: "Its [affect] proximity to the drive impulse [*Trieb*] made it a better pointer to drive activity" (1977, 139). Yet, Freud's views on feelings were significantly different and not as clear. In that regard he says: "We then come to speak, in a condensed and not entirely correct manner, of 'unconscious feelings,' keeping up an analogy with unconscious ideas, which is not altogether justifiable. Actually the difference is that, whereas with *Ucs.* ideas connecting links must be created before they can be brought into *Cs.*, with feelings which are themselves transmitted directly this does not occur. . . . Even when they [feelings] are attached to word representation, their becoming conscious is not due to that circumstance, but they become so directly" (Freud 1923b, 22–23). There is no doubt that feelings, in that statement, belonged to the system *Pcs.* (the repressed), because they have to be conscious and judged first to justify repressing them, then it becomes possible to *di*-repress them later.

There is another feature of affect as a structure within the system *Ucs.* Freud said: "the unconscious speaks more than one dialect" (1913j, 177), which means that the same things in the system *Ucs.* could take different forms. The *Triebhaft* energy is unbound and binding it requires it to become associated with a chain of representations—hopefully the right one that could express it properly. Since this is not the case most of the time, if ever, binding affect happens through a chain of representations that could use different signifiers, like pain being signified by deprivation or demand. Hamlet's rage was signified for a long time in the Shakespeare play by indecisiveness. This feature made Freud discard the theory of the "strangulated" feeling early because he realized that there is no specific affect associated, in an intrinsic way, with any particular representation. Symptoms reveal the arbitrary and provisional links between affects and their representations; therefore, their representation is expected to be the same, also arbitrary. In hysteria affect is converted and represented in physical manifestations or symbolic acts. In the obsessions, affect is displaced and dissociated from its representations, and sometimes is reversed. Freud acknowledged the possibility for affect to be completely repressed (Freud 1915d), but will always leave a sign of its absence.

Free association, as the psychoanalytic method and technique, is the only means by which we can uncover the ontogenesis of the unbound affect, which has gotten bound to representations in confusing ways. In other words, affect remains unconscious material until we follow its unique web of word representations through a net of signifiers, because it goes through transformations, representations, and representation of representations of unknown and unspecific nature. It takes some time to listen attentively to the implicit metaphors in the patient's speech to recognize the point of fixation that those metaphors are emanating from. In its transformations, whether it takes the form of feelings, symptoms, acts, ideas, phantasies, or transference, affect remains unconscious, and only interpretation could gradually reveal its signification. *Clinically, making the unconscious conscious is tracing a representation as close as possible to its origin through the workings of the primary process.*

Ignoring the distinction between the two conceptions of affect and feeling leads to misconceptions of other important phenomena in analysis. Arlow and Brenner (1964) considered the absence of affect in the analytic situation a manifestation of resistance and defense. They considered the lack of emotional tones in transference a manifestation of limited enactment of the relationship with the analyst. Notwithstanding, affect does not appear as is and always materializes as a representation (feeling is only one). Therefore, it should be there in every analytic setting but not always as emotion. We should not consider the absence of feelings in transference a form of defensiveness because its lack could simply be the transference of apathetic mothering repeating an emotionless relationship with the analyst. It is the analyst's task to look at it in the context of the process of representation and not resistance, because what is called resistance has no place in a structural theory of psychoanalysis.[2] Limentani says (1977): "The success and failure of an analysis could in fact be said to rest on the degree of affective changes which take place during its course. . . . *A feeling is an affective representation* [my italics], is an *internal* [my italics] rather than an overt activity, yet it is seldom out of touch with the external situation" (172–74). Although Limentani was not addressing the psychology of affect separately from the phenomena of feelings, he made it clear that what should change in psychoanalysis is not affect and its feelings but the link between affect and feelings. The problem with affect stems from a common misconception shared by many analysts, and stated succinctly by Arlow, when he said (1977) that Freud: "Found it very useful to separate the feeling tone—or affect as it came to be called from its concomitant or associated ideational content" (157). Separating affect from its content was *Freud's discovery and not a chosen and preferred measure of theoretical expediency*. This separation is what led Freud a little later to distinguish primal repression from repression proper.

Neglecting the distinction between the two conditions manifested in the prevailing neglect of the difference between systems *Pcs.* and *Ucs.*

Pulver (1971) said: "Since unconscious in the descriptive sense includes preconscious, let us begin with some evidence of preconscious affect" (350). Freud was clear about that matter and dealt differently with affect and feeling in terms of their conscious/preconscious and unconscious states. Missing this point made Pulver say: "Unconscious affect consists of situations in which the individual shows physiological, ideational, and motor behavior usually *associated* with *a central feeling state* [my italics]" (Ibid., 351). The distinction between affect and feeling entails a distinction between the preconscious and the unconscious (aconscious), which is clearly of significant importance in psychoanalysis.

Freud's distinction between the endosomatic and exosomatic (external) simulations is more than just identifying the source of the stimuli. The endosomatic stimuli are not perceivable or conceivable and are all experienced as affect: pleasure or pain. An ideational representation of that affect is supposed to initiate the identification of the stimulus: hunger, sleepiness, constipation, etc. But without sensory organs or guidelines in the infant's mind of differentiating between the endosomatic stimuli identifying the stimulus has to come from the mother. It starts with providing the infant with the objects of his need (breast, pacifier, support for other needs, etc.) followed gradually by the verbal equivalent of those needs. So, the first representations are initiated by the mother and are concrete representation (thing representation), ensued by word representation (symbolic or word representation) (Freud 1915c). The process of representation thus depends on the mother's empathy, ability, maturity, and transparency, if not her own psychoneurosis, because she will improvise the first representations of the infant's affect. The mother is the first builder of the intrapsychical structure of the infant; a deed that would no doubt be influenced by her relation to her baby. However, the mother-child situation becomes the field of mutual expressions and language.[3] In other words, the mother structures the infant's intrapsychical, and the intrapsychical relates (talks) to her and all others after. Object relations are the attestation to the existence of an intrapsychical core that initiates the relationships.

The absence of distinction between affect and feeling could seem inconsequential if it is not put in its proper perspective. As affect is the antecedent of feelings and the chain of subsequent representations, it should be emphasized that the origin of affect is not a matter of theoretical preference or choice. The origin is *Trieb*: *the human version of the natural urge to react to internal stimuli,* which is transformed spontaneously—in humans—into a psychical condition of a mental potential. There is no other mechanism known to us psychologists that explains that process. *Trieb* is a peculiar conception in psychoanalysis, because it was the least significant concept to most of the old generation analysts, including some of Freud's contemporaries. Most ardently orthodox analysts could disregard it without any obvious signs of deviating from orthodoxy. Yet,

Freud considered *Trieb* "the most important part but at the same time the least complete of the psychoanalytic theory" (1905d; 1924f, 168). Every time Freud came to a new understanding of clinical material or had a theoretical insight which required revision of the theory, he went back to *Trieb* and modified it to tally the new modifications. The best example is the period between the introduction of narcissism (1914c) and the conception of the *repetition compulsion* (1920g). During that time Freud paid attention to the vicissitudes of the instincts (1915c) and came to grips with the significance of the aggressive component in melancholia (1917e), and unexpectedly he replaced the conception of fixation with that of repetition compulsion. As a result, the theory of *Trieb* changed radically to fit in the new discoveries. The sexual versus self-preservation duality was replaced with the quality of life and death

Therefore, *Trieb* is not a functional conception in the theory of psychoanalysis; it is not the product of a certain theoretical conviction, but a conception that has structuring implications. It is a conception that reflected the nature and course of psychical development and proved necessary to keeping the three defined metapsycholgies interdependently linked and interchangeable too. What is of special importance is the fact that the conception of *Trieb* did not instigate change, and when it was subjected to change, the change was in its content and not in its structural nature. It remains *the measure of the pressure put on the mind to act; it came in dualities not plurality and its duality was dialectical not conflictual.* This simple fact clearly suggests that Freud was concerned with the antithetical elements of the *Trieb* and not their conflictual nature, or with their behavioral manifestations. It is unfeasible for a conception of that nature to create a psychology of its own, a psychology of *Trieb*, or a drive psychology as the contemporary schools define psychoanalysis.

Psychoanalytic thinking is characterized by the adeptness to deal with two meanings in anything said or done. When the analyst listens and analyzes a representation he knows that he is dealing with a secondary meaning of a primary issue lurking behind the patient's speech. The structural theory stipulates that what we deal with is product of the primary process, which never ceases affecting psychical life and though unconscious it engenders endless forms of its source. The analyst knows that the secondary forms do not preclude the existence of the primary origin. The primary is always operating in every transformation of the affect into its representation (see chapter 3).

METAPSYCHOLOGY, PHANTASY, AND THE PRIMAL

Freud insisted until the end that metapsychology is essential to psychoanalysis. Just two years before his passing he said (1937c): "Without metapsychological speculations and theorizing—I had almost said phantasyzing—we shall not get another step forward. Unfortunately, here as elsewhere, what our Witch reveals is neither very clear nor very detailed. We have only a single clue to start from—though it is a clue of the highest value—namely, the antithesis between the primary and the secondary processes; and to that antithesis" (225). Metapsychology constituted a problem in psychoanalysis: What is its function? Answers from the critiques of metapsychology attest to the vagueness of its connotation in the minds of psychoanalysts, and to some extent Freud's own mind (Rappaport and Gill 1959).

Home (1966) and Bowlby (1981) considered metapsychology the scientific basis of psychoanalysis, differentiating it from the therapeutic aspect. It was considered, thus, an abstraction of the clinical findings that is distinct from the theory. Mackay (1981; and Meltzer 1978) did not find a useful function for metapsychology in object relations theory. There are no metapsychological formulations that accommodate the subject matter of object relations theories. Metapsychology relates (though indirectly) to "psychologies," and relations have no psychology as the elements of the intrapsychic have. Metapsychology constituted a problem of a different kind to ego psychology. Ego psychologists depended completely on Freud's structural theory (1923b). It was considered an elaboration of the topographic point view, and thus dismissed the economical and dynamic points of view as redundancies (Arlow and Brenner 1964; Brenner 1980; Hartman 1948; 1964; Gill 1979; Rappaport 1951). Strange enough, doing away with the topographic point of view in favor of the structural point of view necessitated dismissing—as irrelevant—the distinction between the *Ucs.* and the *Pcs.*, Eliminating the distinction between the two systems of unconsciousness and precociousness eradicated the need for a concept of primary process. The psychology of the ego was soon found out to be extremely wanting: What is the value of a psychology *the pronoun of the first person singular?* As the crisis of ego psychology without metapsychology threatened to collapse, a new plea emerged: modernize and replace the three old points-of-view with new ones. For instance, Holt (1965a, 1965b) suggested replacing the economic point-of-view with a theory of communication. Prior to that there was the movement to eliminate the topographic point of view completely. The movement to modify or change metapsychology failed badly, but was followed by a call for separating theory from the practice of psychoanalysis.[4] This call implied, in a clear way, that psychoanalysis should have a clinical theory, leaving the theoretical "theory" to non-clinicians.

The efforts to rid psychoanalysis from metapsychology took another peculiar form. A number of analysts considered metapsychology unrelated to psychoanalysis and only a reflection of Freud's educational and professional background. Therefore, it was sometimes characterized as neurophysiological (Rubinstein 1997), biological (Holt 1965a), mentalistic, vitalistic, dualistic (soma/psyche), physicalistic (causative), and hermeneutic. Those attempts took on a life of their own and were irrelevant to both the clinicians and the theoreticians and were considered extratheoretical in nature (Ellman and Moskowitz 1980). There were other attacks on metapsychology based on philosophical "accusations" like being Cartesian, Kantian, Husserlian, etc. A last attempt was to go straight to replacing metapsychology with better metapsychlogies. It was suggested to use the term appetite to replace *Trieb* (Holt 1976), self-organization instead of ego (Klein 1976), cybernetic feedback to mean affect (Rosenblatt and Thickstun 1997). The final say about all that is a question: What was the reason, the justification, the drive behind getting rid of metapsychology in psychoanalysis? Meissner (1979a, 1979b) underscored the fact that no suggested solution or vocabulary was equal and adequate to justify eliminating metapsychology from psychoanalysis.

The failure of all those unexplained endeavors to demise metapsychology revealed an aspect that was not clear before their failure. Metapsychology is the best way to speak of the psyche of the individual and the human psyche in general in the same language and using the same vocabulary. Better, metapsychology allows using the same conceptions in explaining the individual unit and the general phenomena, e.g., the hysteric and hysteria. *It is a bridge between the informative theory (the individual) and the structural theory (the phenomenon), because as a meta-psychology it deals with shared originator or the representation of affect.*

It is imperative to consider the material that we deal within analysis representations first; representations of affect second; and has arbitrary links with affect third. It is imperative to keep that in mind lest we get tempted to interpret the material as set entities or "givens." For instance, if we do not keep that configuration in mind we would be tempted to understand a negative transference as an aggressive attitude toward the analyst. But aggression toward the analyst is transference in the first place, and transference is a representation of something that happened before it became a hostile feeling; then we need to know how and with whom it got into that state. For example, a very cooperative female patient was going through a difficult divorce in which she needed annulment of the marriage. She was seeking her father's influence to get the annulment and he was showing hesitancy because of his own religiosity. She became aggressive and belligerent with me (her analyst) and decided at one moment to end her analysis. My first understanding was breaking up with me as acting out a difficult divorce; an understanding based on the similarity between two givens: breaking a relationship with an ineffective husband and a transfer on an ineffective analyst. A few months later she sked to resume her therapy and she did. She got her divorce while she was back in analysis. She explained her impatience with her analysis as being upset because things were not working well in her life and with her analysis. She mentioned that she was very angry at her father in particular because during that period she felt that he was punishing her for her marriage, which he did not approve of in the first place. His hesitation in getting her the annulment was seen as his revenge. Ending the analysis was transferring her revenge from him to me because she felt we were both having what she wanted and we were exercising our authority over her. Previous memories that were mentioned in her analysis about her early relationship with her father and his favoring of her brother over her got a good chance to be reconstructed. This is a tendency easily recognizable in the contemporary schools of psychoanalysis and psychotherapies, because they take object relations (with their strong affective-feeling and emotional mix) as entities that need to be explained without first analyzing them to their origins in the intrapsychical structure of the persons involved.

In this vignette it is clear that we are dealing with the working of the primary process in a way that we cannot specify without the help of metapsychology. The patient's marriage was influenced by the transformation of her feeling of frustration about her father's treatment into a desire to hurt him. The conscious linked with a series of preconscious memories became a constant pressure that kept getting stronger by the unfulfilled wish. Her marriage represented the dynamic setup of narcissistic injuries, some from the past with the father, some from the present with the husband, and topped by the analyst's place in the conflict. The preconscious anger linked with the aconscious hurt to form a conscious act of rebellion. The dynamics of that set-up changed to a narcissistic hurt, because her failure to get the annulment meant victory to her husband. Narcissistic hurt set up, by means of metonymy, a new dynamic: the one who asks and the one who is not getting what she asks for. Economically, and under the dynamics of the metonymy, the pressures of the psychoanalytic situation allowed making it a scene in which the conflict is enacted.

Metapsychology in the English school of object relations was at least ignored and at most rejected. The Kleinians preferred dealing with feelings (defined and qualified emotional condition) over affect (a state of unidentified mood) for two reasons. First, giving the unconscious a content that determines the nature and quality of relating to the object facilitated bypassing the intrapsychical contribution in establishing the object relation. The second reason is making feelings the quality of the unconscious and changing the *Ucs.* from a system dominated by the primary process into an entity that is dominated by fantasy, which takes a prominent place in transference and countertransference. The ideas of "projective identification" (Klein 1946; Heiman 1950; Ogden 1986), the "container and the contained" (Bion 1963), and the "holding environment" (Winnicott 1955), etc., are based on some sort of "feeling someone else's feeling" (note that one cannot "feel" the effect of another but maybe could recognize his feelings). In this context, feelings were seen as fixed structures within a situation that could be reactivated—as is—in another situation (in the transference). This proposition of object relation depended on the phenomenon of feeling, and would not have had a place for a proposition of affect, which is contingent on representation (Green 1977). It was logical and justified that object relationists called for separating the art of therapy from metapsychology.

As metapsychology bridges the informative and the structural theories, it also distinguishes between the primary and the primal. When we talked about the difference between those two conceptions (chapter 3) the emphasis was on the place of the originator in each. The primary is a psychical phenomenon that is a product of the system *Ucs.*; it is product of an aconscious process. It does not have a conscious form, but as non-repressed unconscious (Freud 1923b) it is active and forces noticing its presence and its significance in understanding certain psychical phenomena. Our conscious thinking is impossible to comprehend if we do not recognize the overlap of two processes: a primary process which its main interest is to represent the endosomatic in a mental form and a secondary process that tries to adjust those representations to the principles of the external world that will respond to them. This complex relationship between the two processes can only be expressed metpsychologically, as Freud suggested in his aforementioned statement. The endosomatic originator of the act of representation is aconscious, needs to link with something(s) related to consciousness, and that link would be by definition preconscious. The endosomatic, which is *Trieb-like,* depending on the degree of pressure (economics), will show more of its primary nature, thus will engage in psychodynamic balancing act to be represented in a conscious form.

FANTASY, THE PRIMAL, AND AFTER-EFFECT

The concept of *Trieb* was pivotal in the debates, arguments, and eventually the disintegration of the classical theory. The reason is translating it by instinct and the absence of credible correction of that major mistake. This translation sent analysts off course making that psychical life seemed to be instigated by "drives" instead of the pressure of the endosomatic on the mind to start the process of representation and creating the systems of *Cs., Pcs.,* and the *Ucs.* However, Hartmann (1948) changed *Trieb* to mean instinctual-drive, then simply called it "drive" by eliminating the term instinct. Holder (1970) has shown that Freud used *instinkt* in only five of his works, and when he used instinct it meant the inherited potential which deals with the external world in a predictable way, and is encountered only in animals.[5] Nonetheless, it did not take time or effort for the term instinct to raise questions about psychoanalysis as a drive psychology. This change created two problems: the disappearance of the conception of turning the endosomatic into a representation and giving birth to psychical phenomena, and using drive as the original Freudian term, although drive is linguistically misleading.[6] Dropping the proposition *Trieb* is significant as it is, because it represents what plagued the theory of psychoanalysis.

Mistranslation, misconceptions, minor modifications, and changes to the original theory were done sometimes frivolously, causing major distortions to the information the theory delivered. Missing the contradiction within those revisions, the prevalence of the informative theory created "irresponsible" criticisms of psychoanalysis. Thence, the whole theory was gradually considered flawed. Going through some of those critiques is useful in finding our way back to the original doctrine and from there to future psychoanalysis and the psychology of the subject.

Misconceiving psychoanalysis as a drive psychology has produced the notion that if mental activity is initiated by a somatic change it has to finish with somatic change. To some, this meant that psychoanalysis is not a psychological theory (Compton 1983, 381). It was also believed that a conception of *Trieb* forces us to deal with the dichotomy of body/mind in a way that does not concern psychoanalysis. Compton stated this idea by saying (1981): "[To] understand the theory of drives . . . , it is necessary to understand [its] constraints. They consist of Freud's excitation theories, transposed from a neurological to a psychological context, his early ideas on sexuality, and the topographical model of the mind. The problems of excitation theories and Freud's early ideas on sexuality are part of the general problems of mind-body relationship" (192). There is no way of getting away from the idea that even psychological phenomena must have some excitatory origin. The endosomatic excitation, which is the inevitable result of the continual homeostatic imbalances, was what Freud meant by the state of affects (pleasure or pain). Freud viewed it as the starting point in the representational process: a non-somatic process, and the source of all ensued psychical phenomena. Therefore, the endosomatic excitation in the Freudian doctrine was, in every sense of the word, the proper solution to the Cartesian dichotomous proposition of body and soul, which later was changed to mind/body dichotomy. Freud said that the pressure of the body transforms into something psychological, i.e., the body is transformed into mind so that the subject would act upon its demands. The proposition of the libido was the metaphorical expression of what moves the mind to deal with the body.

The claim that Freud's idea of the endosomatic origin of psychical activity has to end in somatic change is a grave misconception. Freud said (1894a) that "in mental functions something is to be distinguished—a quota of affect or sum of excitation—which possess all the characteristics of quantity (though we have no means of measuring it), which is capable of increase, diminution, displacement, and discharge, and which is spread over the memory—traces of ideas" (60). This clearly means that the discharge of the "quota of affect" in a somatic manner is only one of the channels available to *Trieb*. However, if—as the critics of the theory of drives insisted—the phenomena we deal with are somatic and their change has to be somatic too, then the somatic must be taken as a drive in the narrow meaning of a *fixed entity*. Hunger would be satisfied by eating and sex by intercourse, etc. But we (analysts) know that hunger could create revulsion to food and that eating is not always instigated by hunger, as sexual arousal is not always extinguished by sexual acts. Infantile sexuality reveals that sex is not an urge and excitement but a manifestation of the libido's plasticity and capacity to take all sorts of forms and representations. Infantile sexuality and the arbitrariness of representing the endosomatic stimulus challenge Cameron's reasoning of labeling psychoanalysis a "drive psychology."

Another source of the argument of drive psychology came from a blatant misunderstanding of what is called "the model of the hungry baby." In *The Interpretation of Dreams* (1900a), Freud used the example of a hungry baby to stage the topographical model of the mind, and to describe the process that instigates the development of the psychical apparatus. Hunger makes the child uses his thumb to recall the pleasurable feeling of sucking the breast. The experience of pleasure instigates psychical processes of recalling it, i.e., memory. Although he went back to that example only once more eleven years later, in his paper on the *Two Principles of Mental Functioning* (1911b), this model became, as Rappaport (1951) put it "the propositional model of psychoanalysis" and to Safouan (1983) "Freud's epithet of [his] metapsycholgies." That model has far-reaching implications about the issue of metapsychology and psychoanalysis itself, but for now I will limit it to the issue of the place and meaning of fantasy (fanaticizing pleasure) in the structural theory of psychoanalysis. The impotence of examining the concept of fantasy and its place in the classical theory is delineating the difference between the classical theory and theories that have no psychologies, which in turn do not require metapsychlogies like the theories of "relation-alties."

Fantasy is an embedded concept in the example of the hungry-baby. Freud used that example to formulate a model of the onset of psychical life in a bay, and it came five years before introducing the proposition of *Trieb*. It was used simply to show how parting from the biological needs creates the cleavage between the two psychical systems of *Ucs.* and *Cs.* The 1911(b) paper was about the emergence of one principle from another, *reality emerging from the pleasure-pain states*. It was about the birth of the function of "attention," leading to the formation of fantasies, memory, and thinking in that sequence. The reality principle was seen as a product of the pleasure/pain principle and not as its antithesis. It also emphasized that "psychical reality" is a natural extension of the pleasure principle, and belongs to the gap between the *Ucs.* and the *Cs./Pcs.* systems. It is the link that allows the aconscious to seep into consciousness. It is important to highlight that "reality" in psychoanalysis is not the "material reality" that is usually called external in contrast with an internal reality (psychical), and is not the spontaneous product of the perceptual-sensory organs, as well. The main trend in psychoanalysis is to put psychical reality in divergence with physical reality. This contrast resulted in making what is psychical a distorting factor in conceiving external reality. Psychical reality in many psychoanalytic writings has a major role in creating the psychoneuroses. Moreover, fantasies are considered byproducts of the unconscious processes or the corollary of the unconscious. Spillius says: "Basically Klein's view, as expressed by Isaacs is that unconscious fantasies are 'the primary content of unconscious mental processes,' the mental corollary, the psychic representative of instincts. Fantasies are the equivalent of what Freud meant by the 'instinctual representative' or the 'psychic representative of an instinctual drive'" (1992, 5). This same distinction was made previously by Freud (1916–1917) saying: "Phantasies possess *psychical* as contrasted with material reality [for] . . . *in the real world of the neurosis it is psychical reality which is the decisive kind*" (368). There is a flaw in those two conceptions of psychic reality and phantasy as its corollary, because the only reality we have is psychical reality. External reality has no independent existence before psychical reality latches onto it: the anatomical difference between the sexes becomes a reality only by virtue of the psychological conflicts in the Oedipus familial structure, and not before. Analysts confuse phantasies with psychical reality.

Freud's placement of fantasy within psychic reality suggests that psychic reality has more to it than fantasies. He implicitly regarded psychic reality parallel to material reality, as if they coexisted in the individual's mind. In other terms, Freud's abovementioned statement suggests that an individual might react and respond to the so-called material reality in a manner comparable to psychical reality. People respond to the news of war as news of material reality, but within their own "proclivities" toward the side they are supported in the war. Similarly, a cigar is a cigar but one might smoke it for pleasure and another for arrogance (making it something else). Those two misconceptions about psychical reality and few more derived from regular clinical experience allow us to find out that fantasy is merely *one* of the responses instigated by psychical reality. In the aforementioned case of the divorcing female patient her responses and reactions to the scene of analysis were to a phantasy that the analytic situation replicated the *external* situation she had with her father and her husband. Her fantasy was the proper response to a sense of frustrating reality, without which the analytic scene would have not become a therapy scene. The phantasy replicated a so-called material reality of a certain kind of frustration. The material situation of frustration was, in essence, a psychological reality. Frustration with the analytic scene was phantasmic, preconscious, and not unconscious as the Kleinians would propose.

We should not forget that there are no unconscious fantasies because there are no conscious phantasies. Daydreams are not fantasies and are usually the proper response to frustrating material reality. The Kleinians had to develop their own theory of the unconscious, which was based on Freud's dynamic concept of the unconscious. It was necessary for the Kleinians to consider the unconscious a psychical entity which is made of contents that are in a dynamic state (but not id content). They looked for corollaries of the *Trieb*, like fantasies, to stand for the unconscious. The reason for preferring such replacements is not as simple as it might look. In Freud's theory of *Trieb*, fantasies are one of the representations of the *Trieb*, and by definition products of the unconscious. Fantasy in the classical theory is a product of the unconscious while in the Kleinian theory it is the unconscious or the shape the unconscious takes. A Freudian analyst deals with fantasy as one of the vicissitudes of the *Trieb* and would look for the unconscious mechanisms that structured it, contrary to the Kleinian who would consider it an embedded element in the object-relation. In the object-relations theories the relationship with the object has as its core an unconscious fantasy. For instance, a patient was compulsively inclined to "think" of what others think of her even if it was just a passing relationship. If we take to the original Kleinian proposition, the patient's thought would be considered manifestations of an unconscious fantasy pertaining to an earlier relationship with an object. In classical terms, the compulsion to think of nothing else in the encounter with the other than the relationship itself is the issue. To that patient, encountering an other had one meaning: How am I seen by him or her? It depicts an intrapsychical structure that has no place for the other in it except as a mirror (remember Narcissus). *The actual conflict in an individual's life is not between the pleasure principle and reality principle, or between fantasy and reality, but between psychical reality and fantasy, where fantasies which are stunted psychical realities could interfere with the resolution of that conflict.*

In "therapy," we try as psychoanalysts to bring psychical reality out of its preconscious disguises in order to make it available for conscious awareness and rework its primary process's distortions. We do not do that with the intention of eliminating it, or to make it subordinate to the "other" realities. It is incorrect to think that psychical reality is projected on the "other" reality (it happens only in psychosis), therefore it spoils it. Psychical reality, although it links with physical reality, does not distort reality except under certain and unusual conditions. The proof of that is the limited sphere and time that physical reality is affected by the neurotic's psychical reality. The neurotic awareness of the imprecision of his conception of reality is an additional proof that psychical reality could link pathologically with aspects of other realities but does not project on the rest of the other reality.

Because the subject has to deal with physical reality in a psychological fashion and that part of his psychical reality could generate phantasies, we find ourselves dealing with two of the most important subtle and structural conception that Freud came up with: the *primal* and after-effect. They are neglected by theoreticians and almost ignored by the clinicians. The primal (primal father, primal phantasy, etc.) is a representation of an originator the left behind its sequels, thus its representation is distant from the originator but remains linked to it in a chain of metaphors and metonymies. Although most of the primal phenomena came to Freud from the social area, he realized that some of the most significant representation in the individual have the quality of the primal—they clearly insinuate that they are sequels of something primal. As an example, Freud talked about primal phantasies, which are in Laplanche and Pontalis's words (1973): "Typical phantasy structures (intra-uterine existence, primal scene, castration, seduction) which psychoanalysis reveals to be responsible for the organization of phantasy life, regardless of personal experiences of different subjects" (331). His concept of the primal agrees with the *Ucs.* as structure and a system and not a function and a content. Moreover, it is structural in its nature and applies to both the individual and the societal. A male dominated society functions unconsciously according to the laws of the primal father, and precociously endows (cathects) the religious institution with the moral authority of the archaic father creating stale social dynamics that praise tradition highly. The same terminology (metapsychology) applies to the fundamentalist and the traditionalist in any society. Metapsychology is very useful in identifying what would be talked about in that regard. The concept also explains something about phantasy that could easily be missed. Phantasies could be the organizing force of psychical reality. Clinically, it is intriguing to notice that the main metaphoric forms the patient seems to prefer relate to his bodily functions, but, they come through as being processed in a specific personal way. The concept of a primal phantasy seems to be relevant in that respect.

The second concept of after-effect needs some qualifying explication. The *Irma* dream (Freud 1900a) instituted the notion that for a psychical phenomenon to happen there should be a link between the present event (day residual) and a related past event (childhood wish). Rarely did analysts asked why that is so, although the informative theory is full of reminders about this feature in our psychical life. Childhood sexuality and symptom formation, fixation and regression, trauma and precipitating factors, childhood experiences and transference, and a few more links corroborate the significance of the after-effect concept. The structural significance of that concept is in making the analyst aware that whatever material he is analyzing, it is made up of two events or more and not only the one the patient avers. Moreover, the work of analysis is to discover the structuring process that linked those events. Without the concept of after-effect the basic proposition of the unconscious would be useless, unusable, unpsychoanalytic, worse, or non-existent. The structural quality of the concept of after-effect engrains in the analyst the sensitivity to a *lack* in the patient's narrative; the lack is obvious but what is lacked is not.

Future psychoanalysis would not actually come by unless and until present psychoanalysis has gone out of our system of thinking. It is not a simple uncomplicated matter to waive current psychoanalysis out and replace it with a new one. However, it seems easier to put aside current psychoanalysis than to replace it. This is already happening subtly as the crisis of the deterioration of the status of psychoanalysis continues, but replacing it is no doubt difficult. We do not have yet a clear complete replacement for it.

NOTES

1. Affect (Affekt) is a sensation that is either agreeable or disagreeable and could be pleasurable or painful depending on the intensity of the sensation. The fact that a pleasurable sensation could turn into a painful one, if it increases in intensity (pain into pleasure in other occasions) confirms that affect is not feeling (gefuhl). Feeling changes qualitatively and not quantitatively.

2. It is important—as we will see in chapter 6—to consider that the affective states of the patients or the lack of them are acquired very early, whether in the transference in the patient's life. Gaensberg infants learn to recognize with exquisite sensitivity the cues indicating changes in the caregiver's quality of responsiveness, at times for life-preserving reasons; infants also develop extraordinary means to facilitate the maintenance of the "good parent" moods. If the intensity of these experiences is such as to massively interfere with their regulation and subsequent integration into a sense of "self as a whole" or "object as a whole," then one tends to see more desperate measures of regulation, such as splitting or "walling off," as I have termed it. This walling off has an adaptive quality, not only in helping to contain the intensity of affect, but also in preventing the traumatic experiences from having as overwhelming an effect on other situations and relationships as they might otherwise have (527).

3. The human infant seems to assimilate the grammar of his "mother tongue" before he learns to speak. He acquires language from his mother's speech before it is practiced in speaking to her. Yet, the affective content of language is predetermined before its ideational content. In other terms, language—for the infant—is not from or a tool of communication, but an invention created by both him and his mother separately from the speaking world. Therefore, it could be said that the infant does not learn language at first but learns his mother's invention of "the mother" tongue. No wonder that whatever the linguistic skills of a multi-linguist person has, his mother tongue is the one he uses to express his intimate feelings and to appreciate humor best.

4. This suggestion differs from Bowlby's and Home's discrimination between the art of therapy and the scientific foundation of psychoanalysis.

5. Freud might have used something indirectly connoting the same thing in thing humans when he talked about the phylogenetic aspect of the human endeavors.

6. Drive is an *external* force that initiates movement by impacting an object, like drive a car or, driving someone to do something; i.e., it does not apply to the spontaneous processing of the act of representation. In the 1920s McDougall established the school of Hormic psychology, or drive psychology which did not meet great success.

FIVE

From the Individual to the Subject

Psychoanalysis—at the present time—is struggling to survive everywhere in the world, but in different degrees of stress. It is in crisis because it is in decline all over the world with—maybe—some signs of vitality in few countries that are new in exploring it, like Eastern Europe and China. Although this conclusion is correct, it is not totally accurate. We have more than one psychoanalysis to presume that they are all in the same or similar predicament. The one most struggling is the classical, because whatever is said about it is still the one that continues to have the distinguished place in the field of the humanities and represents all psychoanalyses to the world. As such, it gets a share of whatever is said about the other theories. Moreover, its international organization has to deal with the chaotic attacks on it from the contemporary schools too, survive as an organization that is still an umbrella for several of those schools, and is basically confused about being a professional organization and an educational body too. Although the crisis of psychoanalysis, as explained in chapters 1 and 2, reached a critical point, identifying its nature is problematic. From the very beginnings the concerns about psychoanalysis were deliberated within the context of its status as a profession. Yet, there was no concern then about the theory and its impact on practice and its techniques. Even when the crisis now manifests in deterioration of the profession of psychoanalysis many analysts are still not looking at the theory as the cause of that deterioration. They maintain the preoccupation with everything related to psychoanalysis except its theory. The crisis has always been expected and worried about but never confronted. But we have come now, after more than five decades of open disagreements, to admit that the old patchwork on the theory is not helping in dealing with the crisis. *What is important about this recent change is the way it happened, because it reveals the basic resistance over the year to see that solution*, and maybe the way toward a solution.

PSYCHOANALYSTS AND THEIR DISCONTENTS

Analysts always believed blindly in the soundness and correctness of psychoanalysis. Jones said (1936): "My mind is literally incapable of imagining the mass of our valuable insight and knowledge vanishing from the earth, so long as any sort of civilization endures. Nor can I doubt that in the course of centuries psychoanalysis, the science of the unconscious, will play an increasingly central part in all studies and activities that have to do with the unfolding of man's mind and the determination of his well-being" (276). It is understandable that in 1936, Jones would see what was in front of him but it is also obvious that he put the emphasis on securing its survival on the status and the reputation that psychoanalysis had. Spruiell (1989) had the same attitude that analysis will survive and mentioned indirectly that the theory has a strong core that will keep it from collapsing. He did not specifically name that core but gave the impression that it has a structural base that would last beyond its informative aspect. However, he suggested two reasons for his confidence in psychoanalysis's survival: it has shown resilience in front of several threatening circumstances before and because it is also needed in the field of human studies. Michels (1988) did not see that psychoanalysis is threatened and pointed out that: "The future may bring a reorganization of its professional institute structure, a strengthening of its scientific base and research tradition, and a shift toward recognizing and integrating the public responsibilities of an organized profession with its traditional primary concern with the value of the individual analyst-patient relationship" (184). He too showed almost blind faith in the survivability of psychoanalysis because he thought that if analysts only paid attention to the discoveries analysis made they will be able to secure its future. Orgels (1990) refers the problem with psychoanalysis to the poor personal psychoanalysis of analysts, otherwise she did not see anything to warrant concern about the future of the discipline. Her conception of the crisis is limited to the quality of the psychoanalysts. Cooper (1990) agrees that changes have to come to deal with the future of psychoanalysis but to concentrate on solving the problems of training and clinical work as the solution. He says: "The three serious problems we face as we look to the future that I have outlined are: (1) to acknowledge that there will be change; (2) to find the ways to recruit bright young talent in our field; and (3) to retain the linkage of clinical experience with scholarship and research" (195). He adds his voice to the group of analysts who do not seem to see anything intrinsically wrong with current psychoanalysis except in some detail like its protocol of training. The reason for the blind confidence in the future of psychoanalysis is clear in the approaches taken by some analysts to bring psychoanalysis to its glorious status. Those authors did not acknowledge or recognize what was wrong with the informative theory, and did not know how to discuss its failings (Cesio 1995).

Another group of analysts took a less dogmatic attitude about the infallibility of psychoanalysis. However, this group of analysts still debated the issue of the future of the discipline of psychoanalysis and not psychoanalysis in itself. Rangell, as early as 1975, found in the emergence of viewpoints such as the genital vs. the pregenital, the intrapsychic vs. the interpersonal, and the other divisions regarding metapsychology a threat to the future of psychoanalysis. His concerns were repeated in some of his works on the current status of psychoanalysis and he made clear (1988) that he disapproves of calling the original theory a classical theory because this gave the impression that psychoanalysis could be something else than the original theory. He expressed his disapproval well by saying (2000): "What I consider the fragmentation of theory, a name I apply in lieu of pluralism, is not an academic subject but a very practical issue. In my opinion, such splintering and its confusing and divisive effects are more responsible for the modern decline in the status and popularity of psychoanalysis than ecological or external etiologies. Partial explanations are considered to be the entire explanatory system" (451). It seems that Rangell was concerned about the theory of psychoanalysis, but since he did not offer a solution for its fragmentation or an account of "the theory" he considered to be psychoanalysis, we have to assume that his concerns were in regard to the history of the discipline of psychoanalysis. Arlow and Brenner (1988) approached the future of psychoanalysis with two pertinent questions: What will the profession of psychoanalysis be like in the future? What will psychoanalytic theories about the mind and about the treatment of mental illness be like in the future? Both are fascinating and important questions, but the answers were disappointing. They answered the first question by discussing the issue of the medical vs. lay analysts, the full-time vs. the part-time analysts, and finally the number of weekly sessions and the length of time that would be accepted in analytic practice. The second question happened to be unrelated to the theory but only regarding what would be taught about analysis. Their point-of-view was seemingly related to the modifications that will be required to preserve the classical theory and traditional psychoanalytic practice. After reviewing the lines of change in the development of the discipline and the science of psychoanalysis, Wallerstein and Weinshel (1989) came to the conclusion that changes have taken hold of training, but the theory is creating uncertainty and difficulty in agreeing on a definition of clinical practice. They advocated—in principle—that plurality is a fact we have to live with. They say: "The uncertainty, of course, is but one aspect of our growing awareness and willing acceptance of our increasing theoretical diversity, a worldwide pluralism of theoretical perspectives, of linguistic and thought conventions, of distinctive regional, cultural, and language emphases in psychoanalysis" (Ibid., 368). Wallerstein, and the IPA behind him, accepted revoking the notion of a unitary theory of psychoanalysis to save the institution from collapsing (2005).

It was not possible to continue ignoring the precarious position psychoanalysis has reached at the turn of the century. Some analysts realized that psychoanalysis needs the support of other branches of the humanities if it is to survive. This trend started by making distinctions between psychoanalysis as science and as an intellectual endeavor. Terms like hermeneutics vs. science were mentioned in regard to two approaches to the identity of psychoanalysis. But two novel terms were introduced to the burgeoning debate about the identity of psychoanalysis: *idiographic* sciences and *nomothetic* sciences. Those two terms replaced almost all the dichotomies that were used before to characterize the dualities that were previously considered problematic. Windelband (2001/1893) classified the sciences into two classes. The cultural sciences classified as idiographic because they are related to individual cases, and seek the laws that govern the particular case in focus. Thus, psychoanalysis is a case in point of an idiographic science because the analytic work pertains to the individual and the laws that govern his psyche. He classified natural sciences as *nomothetic*, because they are based on the laws that govern the phenomenon in general and not its individual condition.[1] Thus, it aims at defining the form or the structure and not the content of the issue in study. However, this dichotomy is misleading when applied to psychoanalysis because psychoanalysis has the same theory for both the individual unit of a human phenomenon and the same phenomenon in its social state. In both cases inductive thinking is the method of approaching the phenomenon. The informative theory of psychoanalysis is an idiographic theory that was used—wrongly but usually unintentionally—as a nomothetic one. The structural theory of psychoanalysis is idiographic too, because it concerns itself with the interrelationships that govern more than one aspect of the psychical phenomena of the human subject. It is the theory that postulates the psychodynamics of the obsessive-compulsive neurosis and not the psychodynamics of the "Rat Man." Therefore, we do not use the deductive method of the nomothetic sciences in studying individual psychical phenomenon, nor do we use it in any endeavour to study the human subject's phenomena.

There is some significant misunderstanding among analysts about the meaning of the two terms; they were taken as replacement for human or qualitative vs. scientific and quantitative studies. They are synonyms of functional (causative explanations) vs. structural (descriptive interpretative). In other words: the two terms do not relate to certain material of research but only to the method of studying that material. Hauser (2002) used the novel terminology of the nomothetic sciences vs. the idiographic sciences to find a solution for lacking confidence in psychoanalysis. He suggests that we need some scientific quantitative research or nomothetic support for our idiographic science of psychoanalysis. He did not specify what the nomothetic sciences would research for psychoanalysis to reach the quantitative proof of its validity, let alone who would be doing that for psychoanalysis. Schachter (2005) expresses the same confidence in the means of "scientific research" of psychoanalytic findings in restoring the credibility of the profession and its therapeutic merits. Richards and Lynch (2008) asked several important questions which reflect the confusion in the field psychoanalysis: Is psychoanalysis a science or an intellectual movement, a therapy or a theoretical system, a social science or a branch of the humanities or the natural sciences. They came to the conclusion that psychoanalysis does not have a clear answer to those questions and it needs input from other branches of knowledge. The most revealing and disconcerting aspect in an extensive literature on the same theme is the analysts' quasi-sense of entitlement to ask other branches of sciences to do their scientific work that validates psychoanalysis. Prelinger expects that psychology would give psychoanalysis a future. He said (1972): "Analytically oriented psychologists can contribute to this, particularly [the influence of psychoanalysis on American psychology] by collecting further observations and conducting more incisive conceptual analyses, and generally by the maintenance of a comprehensive view of man which must guide their observing, treating, and theorizing."

This approach is disconcerting because it reveals a sense of distrust of psychoanalytic work and a sense of helplessness in regard to defending. Bornstein (2007) tried to make comparisons between what he called idiographic psychoanalysis and nomothetic psychoanalysis, suggesting that we could do our own nomothetic studies (he is a psychologist and has knowledge of experimental and academic research). His attempt was built on two points: five propositions derived from the informative theory, and a partial understanding of the two terms of idiographic and nomothetic. Using the informative theory, which is the idiographic side of psychoanalysis, to provide the nomothetic side with propositions for quantitative, scientific, and experimental framework will face a major obstacle: as things stand now in psychoanalysis there is no experimental model that could be used to test any of the theoretical or clinical observations. As well, there is no psychoanalytic observation that could fit the used known experimental model.[2] When the distinction between the two classifications of sciences is not done in a clear way, the result would be a weak argument.

If we go back to the source of the dilemma we realize that enthusiasm about psychoanalysis as a profession overshadowed Freud's continued stress on the analysts' need to widen their cultural scope and include more than psychoanalysis in their erudition. During his time, and in Europe in particular, the regular educational system took care of most of what he aspired for all psychoanalysts. But his recommendation was neglected and psychoanalysts grew more limited in their culture and concentrated on the technicalities of the practice. Freedman (1974) was concerned about the future of psychoanalysis if it would continue in that direction, and predicted that future psychoanalysis would have to pay more attention to its "scientific" importance than its therapeutic procedure to avoid sterility; presumably suggesting more attention to thinking about psychoanalysts than practicing. On the other hand, Richards in his views about the future psychoanalysis had separated the future of practice (the profession) from the future of the theory, and said in regard to the theory (1990): "Analysts tolerate greater revision of psychoanalysis as a theory of the mind than as a theory of therapy" (349–50). But, because he sees psychoanalysis eventually linking up with other branches of science if it is to survive he believed that "in the decades to come, analysts will refine theory by assigning systematic place to biology. This will enlarge their understanding of human development and provide new referents for understanding [regression as reaction to psychoanalysis]" (359). The idea that future psychoanalysis will lose its privileged status as a distinct discipline in its own right is not a new one. Freud and several of his early followers were agreeable to the non-medical and in some cases the non-trained people to practice psychoanalysis if they demonstrated the ability to do that. Since the formation of the International Training Committee, there were restrictions on that liberal attitude but the issue of lay analysts was always in the picture. However, training remained limited to candidates from "recognized" clinical professions. The difference with the current situation that formed in the last two or three decades is the practical need to open the membership to the psychoanalytic organization to non-clinical people. The sensible solution seems to go in the direction of opening psychoanalysis to other sources of knowledge. This idea is supported by Freud's insistence on widening the analysts' scope of knowledge to benefit from other branches of knowledge, but it reveals an important issue about future psychoanalysis.

Freud was initially convinced that the great contributions of psychoanalysis were not going to be limited to its therapeutic endeavors, but would offer new perspectives on child-rearing, education, continuing research, and the broadening and deepening of the social sciences and the humanities. He believed that psychoanalysis would provide related branches of knowledge with new ways of dealing with their subject matter, i.e., that the other branches would open up to psychoanalysis and benefit from it. He was proven right but in a strange way because psychoanalysis was quietly assimilated in those areas, and became an integral part of the medical and cultural sciences, despite the stubborn conviction of psychoanalysts and the analytic organization to embrace therapeutic competence as its main and only responsibility. This development did not hide from some of the pioneers that the related sciences are benefiting from psychoanalysis and advancing toward wider horizons of studying the human subject. They were also cognizant that psychoanalysis has faced some of the limitations and the inadequacies of its informative theory. Thus, there were some pleas to reconsider the strictly clinical formation of the analysts. Eissler was suggesting turning training institutes into academies that teach more than clinical psychoanalysis. He said (1969): "The task that is proper to an Academy of Man, however, is the systematized research carried on by persons who are experts, not only in psychoanalysis but also in the field to which they apply it. Its goal would be the writing of a metapsychology of language, art, literature, music, religion, history—in brief, of all the different fields of the humanities—culminating in a metapsychology of Culture. The bricks with which to construct such an edifice—or, better, the fragments of bricks—now lie about us and only the architect is wanting who will bring them together into a magnificent structure. Such an Academy would then be the keystone of an arch whose beginnings lay in Aristotle's Academy" (460). Kubie (1952) was also suggesting an overhaul of the teaching of psychoanalysis (not training) almost to the order of making the institute an academic institution. Kernberg (2007) strongly suggested integrating the institutes of psychoanalysis in the academic departments of mental health in universities and opening training to more people who might not be accepted for their lack of clinical background. His call for linking training with the universities was not to widen the cultural scope of the candidates but give exposure to scientific methods and research.

Psychoanalysts did not see any harm in linking with academia because they were already the long distinguished faculty in those institutions. They have always believd that they are members of a discipline that is self-contained and they do not need input from outside that discipline. On the contray, for a long time they convinced themselves that they are the ones needed to enrich the other desciplines with their unique theory. This implicit and explicit attitude in the psychoanalytic circles came from what Cornyetz (1966) considered a misunderstanding of a statement by Freud in which he said (1927a): "In psychoanalysis there has existed from the very first an inseparable bond between cure and research. Knowledge brought them therapeutic success. It was impossible to treat a patient without learning something new; it was impossible to gain fresh insight without perceiving its beneficent results. Our analytic procedure is the only one in which this precious conjunction is assured. It is only by carrying on our analytic pastoral work that we can deepen our dawning comprehension of the human mind" (256). Thus, analysts believed that they need nothing outside the practice of psychoanalysis; they forgot Freud's incessant demand that analysts have to enrich their clinical knowledge with cultural erudition. But Cornyetz said (Ibid., 76): "As it turns out, the psychological-explorative attitude is more helpful to the analysand than is the medical-manipulative approach—provided radical change is intended. Radical change is not always permissible as an effect. Psychoanalysis cannot be done where the analysand cannot permit such exploration to take place. This is the point at which a consideration of modified technique conceptually and methodologically begins." Analysts had to reconsider their perception of their discipline. Royden and Astley said (1974): "We have, it is true, made significant beginnings at extending our knowledge and skills and at enlarging our experience beyond the classical, basic, and indispensable therapeutic dyad. For the most part, however, we do not invest much energy or time outside three areas: psychoanalytic practice, teaching and consultation, and the education and training of candidates in our institutes" (578–79). This statement brings us to the very central issue in the resistance to giving up an old demising theory and replacing it with a theory that would take psychoanalysis to a future: *What would be left of psychoanalysis for the majority of the psychoanalysts who are not theoretically inclined if they are faced with requirement of letting go of the present theory?*

Psychoanalysts now face the challenge of having reached the end of its theoretical understanding of the individual. This is evident in three things. (1) The informative Freudian doctrine has offered everything it promised to offer and for the last seven decades there was no extension, expansion, or replacement for it. The classical analysts have nothing else to do but "pretend" that they are looking for its flaws so that they could modify them. (2) The attempts at modifying the theory resulted and are resulting in producing other informative theories that are either dealing with limited aspects of the original theory or aspire in vain to replace it completely. All those efforts did not come close to the comprehensiveness of the flawed theory. (3) Psychoanalysis—distinct from other therapeutic endeavors—is not delivering the therapeutic results it promised before. Psychoanalysts are not the only ones who reached the end of their road, but psychologists, sociologists, political scientists, thinkers, moralists, and all the active human scientists who are preoccupied with the human subject are in the same quandary. All those scientists and thinkers have come to realize is that there is more to the human subject than what they have discovered until now. It is obvious that those non-analysts have no problem acknowledging this fact. Those scientists are widening their horizons, and are communicating with each other. They are moving toward examining the human subject and not just the attributes that make him an individual. They are examining the manner in which those attributes emerge from unknown processes, which need to be discovered by more than just their disciplines. Only psychoanalysts seem to have a problem with breaking out of the confinement of their rigid identity and realize their helplessness in breaking away from their stagnation without the help of other disciplines. Eisold said (2003):"Freud's definition of psychoanalysis as 'a collection of psychological information' led to the establishment of a rigid boundary between psychology and psychoanalysis, which we are only recently coming to dismantle. And his definition of it as a 'treatment for neurotic disorders' led to the virtually endless effort to define a boundary with 'psychotherapy' in the attempt to sustain a privileged apartness. Loosening those boundaries will inevitably bring psychoanalysis closer to the larger worlds of psychology and psychotherapy, relieving it from the contradictions of its superior aloofness. It will also, I believe, help to clarify its primary mission" (557).

The reason psychoanalysts are resisting moving with the flow is the limitations they put on themselves from the very beginning that they are members of a clinical profession. They do not want the face the fact that they are initially mental health providers practicing a designation within one of the six regulated professions in the health act of their country. Psychoanalysis is not a profession. Moreover, psychoanalysts had an astigmatic view of the interest and contributions of the non-clinical scientists and thinkers; a view that did not see clearly what that major body of erudition has found in the theory of psychoanalysis, of which they were oblivious, and could have improved the scope of their profession.[3]

THE LIMITATIONS OF THE PSYCHOLOGY OF THE INDIVIDUAL

Psychoanalysis has changed radically from the time of the supremacy of the classical theory to the current time when it has no theory to identify or define the causes of its decline. Its practice too suffers badly from the absence of a theory of psychopathology or a modality of cure, which were the points of attraction in its past. During the evolution of psychoanalysis its scope widened to embrace more attributes of the individual that do not pertain to the intrapsychical; instead they pertained to the interpersonal and the object relations fields more. The theory—after being an informative theory of the intrapsychic—became a very confusing informative theory of too many unrelated subjects. The troubles of the original informative theory are doubled by including other informative theories that have different vocabularies and grammars.

The classical theory of psychoanalysis under the pressure of the new schools of psychoanalysis changed in a manner that obviates any possible future for it. The subject matter of the theory changed from the individual and what psychoanalysis could say about his attributes (unconsciousness, narcissism, etc.) to a study of attributes that speak about the individual (ego, relationships, analyzability, etc.). Instead of the individual being the subject matter and the attributes are his representations, the attributes have become the subject matter and the individual became appendage to his attributes. Without the individual being the subject matter of the theory it will be destined to either oblivion or mummification (consider Adler's individual psychology 1956, and Rogers client-centered therapy 1951). There is a limit to what we want to add in the future to what we have already discovered about him. The theory of the individual, when it has reached its boundaries and lived its shelf life, should have taken us to where we could go beyond the individual and their attributes. Regrettably, we ended up with caricatures of the original subject-matter of the theory. Regardless of the flaws of the classical theory as a theory of the individual, it was a breakthrough. The revelation that the individual is not really what he appears to be (naturally and not morally) was adopted by the medical profession and by the whole society. The theory of the individual became part of the general social conception of Man, and appeared as if it had found all the attributes that make the individual who he is; it became a theory of content. It was inevitable and expected that disagreements on the signification of that detailed content will occur. The disagreement on the content should not have caused disintegration of the theory because different theories, especially in human sciences, could coexist. The disagreements proceeded first to destroy the content of the theory of the individual, then after some trivial replacement new contents were provided. The provided trivial content ended up becoming the content of worthless theories of psychoanalysis.

The most important misconception in the whole matter is that the content of the theory of the individual, as Freud and the pioneers suggested, was metaphorical of the fundamentals of the human subject. Advancing psychoanalysis beyond the Freudian doctrine should not have been by arguing and disagreeing on the adequacy of those metaphors or replacing them, but was to search for what the metaphor "represented" because we still have no precise idea of what was represented by those metaphors. In the history of the theory Freud used id (it) in four different meanings, creating, thus, a great deal of confusion about the ego, which is another metaphor. Nevertheless, we still have to ponder how did a theory formulated on metaphors endure all that was thrown at it and survive and exist in whatever form it took? The answer was given by Freud in a very incidental way. Jones (1957) asked Freud about the most important of his works. His answer was the book on dreams and the work on sexuality. Freud regarded the two intuitions of infantile sexuality and wish fulfilment as the most valuable. It would be too simplistic to think that Freud condensed all the psychoanalytic discoveries into two dicta: dreams are the golden road to the unconscious and that maturation aims at the supremacy of the genital zone over all the other elements of the sexual urge. These two dicta are (or were) a novel theory of the *individual* because the individuals who came for therapy have difficulties and deviation in those two principal areas of psychical life. Remarkably, apart from the clinical diagnoses of the psychoneuroses it is not difficult to find in all patients a form of inability to deal with their wishes and different signs of suffering from immature means of pleasure. In better terms: a patient is someone who fails to get satisfaction from his attempts at fulfilling his wishes because of having immature wishes or lacks the means to gratify them. Point in fact, as simplistic and one dimensional this statement might sound it is worth examining closely. The individual who seeks psychoanalytic therapy is aware—at a certain level—that his "sickness" is a deviation or a transformation of something basic and common in all humans. Obsession is a deviation of wariness and the inability to bring somethings to its conclusion. The obsessive patient could still be an active responsible person, despite his agony about certain matters. He might also be considered by many as a dependable person. What we deal with is incapacities or unhappiness that could incapacitate, and not disease entities that make a patient sick. What we do clinically—contrary to a common belief—is not curing patients, but adjusting deviations, correcting misconceptions, or restoring damaging changes because psychical sickness is what happens to some basic aspects of human nature. Most of all we have no measure for success or failure in our work. It seems that when we do a good job we deal with something more than what we treat the individual for.

As was suggested before (chapters 2 and 3) the enduring and resilient aspect of theory of psychoanalysis is its structural base. Uncovering the structural base of the two works Freud chose would be very useful in showing the roots of that base in two very early works which constituted a significant part of the informative theory. *The Interpretation of Dreams* sets the focus on the working of the primary process in creating the manifestation of the psychical events, and differentiating between three mental systems that are in constant dynamic interaction. One of the systems, the *Ucs.*, was a major breakthrough because Freud kept changing its connotation reflecting the potentials in the structural theory. Representation is a key conception in the structural theory; hence the theory of dreams stands out as the birthplace of several structural conceptions of psychoanalysis. More significantly, the theory of dreams was a major informative component of psychoanalysis and had a constant impact on psychoanalysis. It was the theory of dreams that put the act of interpretation in its proper place in the technique of psychoanalytic therapy, and introduced it in our daily life as means to *understanding* human behaviors. The link between a wish and its expression of the individual's self is only established if we interpreted the expression; i.e., *induce* it from the expression.

The *Three Essays on the Theory of Sexuality* introduced the concept of *Trieb*. *Trieb* in the theory of sexuality was "the pressure the somatic puts on the mind to act"; it was the conception of the emergence of the psychical from the physiological. Thus, Freud put psychoanalysis out of the ordinary psychological theories of drives, motives, cause-effect explanations, and made it a theory of the formation and transformation of what constitutes the individual. This is why and how he realized that sexuality must be the basic origin of pleasure, or that any pleasure has a link with sexuality. So, pleasure evolves in conjunction with autoerotism. Sexuality is the final form taken by the pleasure/pain principle, thence, the individual acquires a dual nature of demand and representation.

We can now answer the question: What is the theory Freud left us that endured so much and still kept its unique status?

Freud left a theory made of metaphors of the individual, which were new information about the person. The metaphors were a new system of attributes that we were able to use instead of the old, ill-informed adjectives that characterized the human being. The metaphors recognized and acknowledged the dualities in the individual. As he was discovering new attributes and finding the proper metaphors to denote them, psychoanalysis looked like an informative theory in formation. Notwithstanding, he left us a dialectical methodology for investigating psychological phenomena. The metaphors of the informative theory are our roadmap of the search for future psychoanalysis, because they are just the first outcomes of the two propositions of wish fulfillment and the pleasure/pain principle. However, when we use Freud's dialectical methodology and move from the informative metaphors to the structural quality of his two propositions we would discover two things: (1) Psychoanalysis is more than a psychology of the psyche as a final effect of the working of the *Trieb*. (2) The individual is not the subject-matter of psychoanalysis. For example: ego is a metaphor of the person and the part of his psyche that houses consciousness, the component of the self that deals with external stimulation, the coordinator of the link between the id and the superego, etc. Yet, all those matters are indicators of alienation or internal failure of actualizing the self without the help of the other.[4] Therefore, psychoanalysis needs to be looking for what explains alienation in the human subject and not the ego; the process that breeds the ego that is a metaphor of the individual. The psychology of the individual, which is the main topic of psychoanalysis until now, leads us to the limits of the informative theories of psychoanalysis including the informative Freudian theory.

THE EVERLASTING NEED FOR PSYCHOANALYSIS

Even if we restrict our understanding of psychoanalysis to its clinical aspect and ignore the rest of it, we still have to admit that what we do is not cure people but help them to make changes to natural, common, and fundamental aspects of psychical life. Doing that without the pretense that we create something that was not there before analysis, or erase something that was there translates into revealing the narcissistic fallacy generated by alienation. What we do is helping the analysand see that he lived an image of himself that replaced what he truly is. A clinical vignette would explain the difference.

A patient was rigid and mostly concrete in his relationships with others. He was not aware of his reserved manner in relating to people. However, he had an active dream life and reported a good deal of them in his analysis. He started with dreams that were more like comments on events that happened in the day before the dreams, and reflected the same rigidity and concreteness. After almost two years of analysis he reported a change in his dreams. Some dreams started to have some emotional and feelings colorated. He conveid his discomfort with that development. Those dreams became the rule, and gradually he became apprehensive of dreaming because of the upsetting emotional contents. Things got even worse because the emotions they're feeling in the dreams tended to last for a while after waking up. Some of those feelings like being scared or embarrassed would not leave him easily after waking up. Even while dreaming and about to wake up he was anticipating the persistence of the feeling for a while during the day. The patient lived his life before analysis without feelings and emotions not noticing that he was missing anything.

In the old terminology of psychoanalysis, it could be said that analysis weakened the pressure of repression, strengthened the ego, allowed more of the unconscious to become conscious, the intersubjective engagement with the analyst exposed the ability to feel, etc. However, as the analyst who was supposed to have done all that, I can say with a straight face that I did nothing, or at least I did not do that intentionally. I just did psychoanalysis. I pointed out to him that although he is not a very emotional person and does not demonstrate many of his feelings he still reported to me his emotions in different situations either in the form of opinions or even as unusual (to him) reactions. Pointing that out to him introduced the fact of unconsciously revealing himself in unnoticeable ways, in addition to putting him face to face with alienation (a substitute self-image of an unemotional person). After becoming more aware of those two new features in him the time was ripe to suggest that there must be something specific in being anxious about dreaming and feelings within his dreams. To both our surprises he remembered that in his early adolescence he would have a gush of strange emotions that were unrelated to anything in particular, a state that he was always ashamed of after cooling down. This led to other memories that went back to his childhood when emotions and feelings seemed to him to be dissociated from him or any reason that would explain them (he felt strongly about things that did not happen). Analysis advanced from that point to exploring something that is rarely considered, more so in contemporary psychoanalytic theories. How do humans form and acquire their feelings and emotions. Our primary responses to pleasure/pain states engender feelings, emotions, attachments, etc. This link is very elementary and precedes any mentation of those states. Each side of the pleasure/pain equation will generate more elaborate, appropriate, complex, specific, and affective reactions. But, in the early years of life the possibilities of miss-coupling feelings with situations, ideas, and human figures (fathers and mothers) are varied and numerous. When we think of ambivalence we will realize that affective reactions in adulthood are extensions of childhood patterns. Although this is common knowledge, analysts have no explanation of what makes childhood patterns replicate themselves, despite the fact that this is one of the basic and main issues we encounter in our practice. However, because we do not know, and we have no means to know what forms the basics of psychical life, our informative theory has reached the end of its expediency and usefulness. Psychoanalysis has nothing more or new to add to what has been articulated in Freud's doctrine. But psychoanalysis seems to point out that there is more beyond its present usefulness.

The most distinctive characteristic of human sciences is the manner that they evolve and progress. Their progress does not depend on discovering new things, as happens in physical sciences, but on articulating existing phenomena that were not previously noticed, considered, or identified. Thus, their evolution takes the course of mastering the meaning of a certain phenomenon to the extent of finding and deepening its meaning. Doing that would enable articulating the same phenomenon more proficiently. The move from one meaning to the better one is usually intuitive, while discovering a new physical matter is founded on painstaking observation and experimentation. Psychoanalysis articulated well the characteristics of the individual and led us to a new meaning of the individual: he is not only what the used metaphors depict, but he is a unit in a species; he is a human subject who is a very distinctive being. After several decades of explaining the phenomena of the individual and answering the questions thrown at it, the Freudian doctrine uncovered the need to explore what the metaphors produced and articulated. We are now on the doorsteps of formulating questions about the human subject and directing them properly to the appropriate idiographic sciences and scientists who have the means to research them and answer. Future psychoanalysis will pay more and better attention to what is behind the metaphors we are using, forming proper questions to be shared with other thinkers and scientists who are psychoanalytically inclined. Thus, we need to benefit from our practice and pay attention to the attributes that constitute the human subject, and engage other disciplines in searching for the answer to the question: What made the human subject what he is, so that he became the only creature who could be so unique in his own species? Prelinger anticipated that change in psychoanalysis. He said (1972): "In conclusion, I would like to suggest that the future influence of psychoanalysis on American psychology depends on the fruitfulness and fullness of its own development. Analytically oriented psychologists can contribute to this, particularly by collecting further observations and conducting more incisive conceptual analyses, and generally by the maintenance of a comprehensive view of *man* [my emphasis] which must guide their observing, treating, and theorizing"(103). To reach this point in our determination to get psychoanalysis out of its present stagnation it is important to make the distinction between the individual and the human subject more evident.

The basis and foundation of the classical doctrine is that the individual is a final configuration of "a psychodynamic" structure of conflicting urges and counter urges. Hence, it is a theory of catharsis which advocated that expressing those psychodynamic configurations we could affect change. Elaborating on the classical theory and creating new schools was nothing but forming new metaphors of the original metaphors; a process that loses its impetus the farther it separates from the original metaphors. It is self-deceptive to think that adding and accumulating metaphors of metaphors expands, improves, or takes us beyond the limitations of the classical doctrine. The contemporary schools of psychoanalysis did not find anything new about the subject. Reaching the bounds of the conception of the individual makes us realized that what we know is not enough or helpful in itself. We know that the patient (the individual) is unaware of *what* formed his troubling attribute (anxious, despaired, depressed, etc.). Besides, making him become aware of the formation of those conditions does not help do anything about them like the link between aggression and depression. Without becoming cognizant of *how* that formation took shape, he would have only been informed about himself. If and when both analyst and analysand put together the conditions that caused that link—explaining the link—they find themselves face-to-face with a loop: using a theory that tells them what to look for in explaining what they already found out. This is the nature of an informative theory of the individual because the information it covers is always metaphoric (alienations). There is a certain warp in the information about the individual because he is seen—in the psychoanalytic theory—as a person[5] who is not fully conscious of himself, i.e., he is unconscious of part of himself.

Metaphors of the individual are a condensation of meanings and not ontologically psychological entities. When we characterize an individual as depressed we "mean" a condition that comprises several interconnected psychological states manifested as a mood. Realizing that we deal with the individual through metaphors should make the psychoanalyst look *into* the structure of the metaphor and not *at* the metaphor. A metaphor is a manner of speaking of an ontological entity and needs to be referred to that source. Therefore, if the analyst wanted to go beyond—for instance—the psychical ontological entity of "reaction formation" (a metaphor of linking two opposite urges through negation) he would notice that reaction formation is only a detail in the individual's psychical life and just expresses the individual's condemnation of a certain urge or urges within him. In other words, if the analyst is attentive enough to realize that an individual attribute in the patient is merely a detail of that person, he would not stop at that detail—he would search for the human subject that embodies the individual, because that would be the subject or the one who suffers. The individual performs the suffering of the human subject. The human subject is what gives the individual his individuality; the framework of the dynamic structures that is the basis of the classical theory. The difference between the psychoanalysis of the individual and analysis of the human subject could be displayed in a clinical example: an anxious woman, or diagnostically, a hysterical person was anxious because of latent homosexual inclinations. She recalled after a while that she was subjected early in her childhood to some homosexual seduction and experiences that left strong impressions on her. Thus, she knew what and how her latent homosexual preferences were formed. We found out with time that the problem was in her childhood reaction to sexual pleasure, which was generalized to something more intricate: any sexual desire for pleasure was homosexually directed, and other pleasurable sensations were homosexually colored. However, we did not know what in homosexuality caused her anxiety or what made any pleasure take the form of forbidden homosexuality. If the answer is the social disapproval of infantile sexuality and of homosexuality too have forced their repression, and anxiety becomes the reaction to activating them, we would be making two very unpsychoanalytic things: we would foreclose on the psychical problem by referring it to non-psychical origins (worse, to generalized conceptions). The second is isolating the individual from his entirety as a human subject and looking at one of his attributes or just a detail of the whole of him. This woman's homosexuality is just a manifestation of a childhood experiences which had more to them than just some homosexual experiences. We would be then treating homosexuality in an individual while homosexuality is merely a *condition* of "that" human subject.

The Freudian doctrine was originally a theory of the psychoneurotic attributes of individual patients. Freud's uncanny intuitive faculty made him realizes that those pathological attributes are the pathological form of normal and natural conditions, but differ in intensities. He explored and made some very significant reformulations of that insight and brought out the importance of examining the processes that turn the natural into the pathological, or as Westen (1999) says, that we have unconscious processes and not an adjectival unconscious. *Freud suggested a protocol for psychotherapy, a psychopathological modality, and most importantly a psychosexual modality of development. The first two relate to the individual, but the third relates to the human subject.* The "psychosexual" in the modality of development identifies what develops and matures in the human subject: the impact of the somatic needs on the mind and their representations. Future psychoanalysis will be the branch of knowledge that is in a favorite position to formulate the best questions about the human subject, and engage a wide range of thinkers, scientists, and researchers in finding answers to those questions. For instance, the three issues mentioned in the modality of human development (orality, anal-ity, and genitality) are shared with higher primates. What makes them different in *Homo sapients*? What is the significance of the evolution of the individual in an evolving species? The psychoanalysts encounter fundamental attributes of the individual which need to be explained in terms of the creation of the human subject, whom we started to recognize only a few decades ago. Future psychoanalysis will pay more and better attentions to the sources or origins of the metaphors we are using to define the individual. We have to be curious, for instance, about the process in the Broca and Wernicke's areas in the brain which turn a homeostatic imbalance into a verbal representation. We observe people and patients closely and notice their usage of special metaphors which pertain to certain organs or sensations in the body. Wouldn't it be a novel area of psychological inquiry to turn those psychoanalytic observations into three questions: One for the neurologist, one for the child psychologist, and one for the linguist?

THE PSYCHICAL AND THE MENTAL

Although there was an attack on Freud's topographic model and an effort to replace it with what was designated as the structural point-of-view, it is not possible to talk about the transformation of any psychological process without locating it in the topographical metapsychological modality. The transformation of the somato-affective stimulations into psychical manifestations affects and registers in the three commonly known states of mind: conscious, preconscious, and unconscious states. Any transformation in that regard will implicate all three stats.

Psychical material is best expressed in the vocabulary of topography which enabled describing their dynamic interactions. However, those states of mind do not use the same means of expression: some are expressed as *mental* content (*Cs.*), some are expressed indirectly as psychical background for that mental content (*Pcs.*), though by little intentional effort they could become conscious. The rest is unconscious and can only latch to a preconscious expression to have access to the mental or to consciousness. Although psychical material is represented in consciousness as mental content and is prompted by the secondary processes of mentation, the links between the three states of mind are totally dependant on the primary process. Therefore, it is imperative to stop thinking of *Cs.*, *Pcs.*, and *Ucs.* as three distinct mental states of mind—as the psychology of the individual dictates—and relate the whole mental state of mind to the human subject, given that his mind comprises the whole framework of those three states in one unseparated continuum. The process that creates the conscious material of thinking turns anything that affects the mind into what could be metalized as a conscious state. Consciousness is an attribute of the mental. Emotions, feelings, and sensations fall under the term mental, because they are mentation or ideas for thinking. It is equally obvious that mental activity is impossible to emerge in consciousness if it is not identified as the subject's own thinking. In other terms, for any mental activity to take place in the mind it has to be experienced to constitute a state of self-awareness in the form of a psychological condition. The background of any mentation is the psychical condition of the subject, which puts it into a subjective framework. An anorexic woman does not feel hungry; instead she fears hunger. Her fear of hunger is the psychical background of her need for nourishment. Even away from psychopathology, Man does not have an idea or feeling; he has *his* ideas and feelings. The subjective nature of mental processes is the psychological component of consciousness. The psychical could—with some intentional effort—change from being merely psychical to becoming mental: if I am worried about an issue and workup my worry in my mind, I would be doing something mental. Anxiety that could color the background of the mental process could become subject for introspection and conscious concern, the same way a relaxed state of mind at a time of working something mentally agreeable would remain preconscious because it does not constitute a concern. The psychical is unconscious because its link with the mental (consciousness) is decided by the working of the primary process. For instance, a friend was always extremely agitated before meeting his ex-wife. He could not explain the degree of agitation despite knowing that his apprehension was caused by her seeming disrespect of him. One day he remembered in a session with his analyst an event in which his father "lost it" and abused his mother bodily (he heard the scene but did not see). At that time he was torn between being proud of the father for not giving in to his unreasonable wife and feeling aghast at what he did to his mother. He thought that the scene of anxiety in front of his ex-wife—as he understood it—was a repetition of the inability to decide which attitude he should take from her. He repressed in childhood a conscious state of indecisiveness, and dispelling repression brought back what was out of consciousness. Remembering the forgotten does not change anything except that it gives the person ownership of his memory of psychological condition.

However, it is not always possible to change the unconscious psychical state into some mental activity if the unconscious has not separated firmly from its somato-affective origin, which is *aconscious* and out of any possible chain of mentation. In that case, it would still use the body itself (and not a psychical representation) as the means of expression. We find that in the psychosomatic symptoms, e.g., a primitive fear of aconscious abandonment would create symptoms of intestinal disturbance, or a need for affective closeness would result in symptoms of urticaria. It is conspicuous that no contemporary theory of psychoanalysis has a place for psychosomatic disorders or behavioral disorders, because they have no modality of psychological development.[6]

In *The Interpretations of Dream* Freud reports a dream of one of his female patients (the May-Beetle Dream). The patient had a dream about some beetles being crushed, which brought to her mind thoughts about some aphrodisiac powders made from crushed insects. In the course of interpreting the dream the patient reported that: "some days before she dreamt, she was horrified, in the middle of her daily affairs, by a phrase in the imperative mood which came to her head and was aimed at her husband: 'go hang yourself'! It turned out that few hours earlier she had read somewhere that when a man is hanged he gets a powerful erection. . . . Go hang yourself was the equivalent to: 'Get yourself an erection at any cost'" (291).

Consciously, she loved her husband and worried about him and was able to explain that. The dream she had was about aphrodisiacs which led the patient to talk about her sexual frustration. This frustration was pre-conscious, but it latched to the issue of hanging to come to the surface with psychological abhorrence. Repression was undone by the article on erection. The somato-affective stimulus of sexuality was not conscious, was not preconscious (only when repression was alleviated it came disguised in the form of an obsessive imperative); it remained *aconscious*. The somato-affective urge became the psychical background of the conflictual relationship with the husband. Sex as a somato-affective stimulus is a source of psychical transformations from birth, but was transformed over the years *in that patient-subject* into a demand for erection. That demand was not allowable in consciousness for moral reasons or its possible conflict with her affection and love for her husband. The fluid dynamic exchanges between consciousness, preconsciousness, and unconsciousness remain aconscious and maintain their functions as the origin for new and more psychical transformations. This is why Laplanche (1997) says that the unconscious has two registries, and making it conscious does not make it disappear from the other registry.

Analysis is not an act of informing the patient of what he is repressing (telling him about the unconscious). It is the act of changing something preconscious into something conscious (transforming a psychical issue into a mental content) through interpreting the process of transformations, thus revealing to the patient a mental form that was misleading or confusing him about his intended meaning. The woman Freud mentioned in her dream would not have gained anything if she was told that she hated and loved her husband at the same time. She needed to understand that her obsessive preoccupation was a mental transformation of a psychological state of mind that scared her. *We should not miss that this woman's quandary about her obsessive idea could have been a funny joke between a husband and wife in other circumstances.*

The intrapsychical core of the subject illustrates the nature of the links between the three systems *Cs.*, *Pcs.*, and *Ucs.* It is common to see a fluid interaction between the *Cs.* and the *Pcs.* in creative people who generate a great deal of metaphoric and metonymic ideas. But we could also find the same feature in patients who have severe anxiety or phobic personalities but in a loop: a fluid exchange between the unconscious and the preconscious and less fluidity between the preconscious and the conscious. It is noticeable that the majority of people have rigid links between the three psychical systems, in particular, those with religious or political convictions. They show intolerance to disagreement and sometimes become aggressive if a situation requiring flexibility between those three systems-even temporarily. We encounter that same thing in patients who are not suitable for psychoanalytic therapy.

We do not deal with pathological conditions, which psychoanalytic theories could explain, but with distorted links in the chain of psychical transformation in a particular person, that needs to be discovered and examined with and by the subject, in order for him to deal with its distortion. We do not listen to the patient to relate what he says to a prefixed theoretical propositions, but we listen to a subject who misses an aspect of himself which is required for his integration. Politzer's admiration of Freud's psychology, despite his critique, was its adherence to the human subject and not to his attributes: Freud did not interpret dreams but interpreted the dreamers. He said: "Let us open any of Freud's writings: the report is always based on individual facts, . . . the study of the neuroses . . . is like an individual act that we must explain as being individual"(1992/1928, 48–49).

THE PSYCHOLOGY OF THE SUBJECT

The distinction between the subject and the individual is not superfluous in a discussion about present and future of psychoanalysis. The distinction between subject and individual is necessary because we have reached a point where we have different psychoanalytic theories which each define individual in their own way. They are offering different conceptions of the individual which promise to be unique frameworks, in clearer perspectives, made him explainable, and most of all allow us to talk abstractly about all kinds of individuals; something that was assigned before psychoanalysis to morality and vaguely to philosophy. The individual has been turned into an abstraction of himself, and has become a generic human, with only potentials for modification or variations. Analysts ended up talking about the same things differently, giving the impression that those things have different meanings in their theories, but still apply to the individual. For instance, the absence of agreement on what we meant by *splitting* kept analysts talking about an individual who is splitting or is suffering from splitting. But what would split in the individual, when does it happen, and how does the psychical mechanism instigate it. Yet, splitting is a metaphor of separating the good from the bad in relating to the same object; the same psychological condition in any theory of the individual. It is common to hear an analyst saying that the patient resisted his interpretation of the transference. This sentence says nothing about the patient and hardly says anything about resistance and transference. Resistance is a term that describes a psychoanalytic concept, but does not reflect what the human subject lying on the couch is doing or experiencing. Disapproving of an interpretation is a complex state of mind, and is only considered resistance if the patient is disagreeing with something he should have agreed with in the first place but did not. Therefore, the patient's disapproval of the interpretation or his inability to feel his attitude toward the analyst could be something the individual (patient) is doing or refusing to do but as a manifestation of the patient as an individual, but not him as a subject. As a subject the act of disapproving of an interpretation is a psychological phenomenon that has more to it than not accepting the interpretation: sometimes accepting an interpretation is more of a resistance that disapproving of it. Freud almost missed that point when he suggested not to interpret positive transference, and he said (1912b): "Transference to the doctor is suitable for resistance to the treatment only in so far as it is a negative transference or a positive transference of repressed erotic impulses" (105). In a better way: the psychology of the individual concentrates on transference as positive or negative, while the psychology of the subject concentrates on transference as a psychological phenomenon that needs explanation.

What else should we do if not talk psychoanalytically about our patients and their psychical phenomena in general? The immediate answer is do nothing else; just continue dealing and treating the subject as representation of an individual. However, the real question is: could the representation of the subject, or his persona, replace or substitute for the subject himself (could a woman put her make-up on her image in the mirror and expect to look pretty). Nevertheless, our knowledge of the constituents of the human subject is tentative and at best incomplete to claim that we could move from talking about the individual to talking about the subject. The points that distinguish the subject and the individual belong to the structural theory of analysis, not the functional theory. They are not articulated properly or enough to attract attention yet. Most analysts are grappling with issues which still belong to some functional aspects of the psychological phenomena, which are very distant from their structural base. The human subject knows at a certain level that he is an image of himself and that image—accurate as it might be—is still not he himself. The alienation of the subject in the individual that represents him seems, by all possible means, the natural course of things and is not an option. For instance, most analysands cannot avoid talking about themselves as if reporting on someone else. Functionally speaking, this clinical fact is a big issue because it is perceived as *caused* by identification with someone else. Structurally speaking, the issue of identity is looked at as psychological happening that requires understanding, since it is the natural course for the subject's existence. It is true that most of the time the subject, having failed to assume his true identity, makes himself believe that his image is he himself.

Psychoanalysts need to know how the newly born infant becomes the self-aware person that we all are supposed to be (Stechler and Kaplan 1980). The individual's self-awareness is predisposed to fallacies due to his inability at the very start of the process to free himself from alienation in his image; an image imposes on him. But, since all human individuals are alienated in an image that is not wholly of their making, what and how are we going to reach the subject who is supposed to be an authentic image of himself? What happens to the normal and natural process that results in the alienated sense of self? If we manage to get answers to those questions could we then have a different theory of psychoanalysis and consequently a different clinical practice? In other words, should we aspire and aim at a future psychology of the subject, which will generate a new psychoanalysis?

Answering those questions, which impose themselves on future psychoanalysis, has to be a collaborative work of several branches of the humanities. Neurology is already seriously involved in studying consciousness and several of its derivatives, which should be better conceived in the psychoanalytic theory (see Fayek 2014). Psychology needs a good framework provided by psychoanalysis to adjust child studies to better angles of infant observations. Thinkers are aware of the significance of the gap between the subject and his representation as an individual, yet the issue of authenticity is looked at from the ontological point of view when it has a psychological side to it. Linguists would benefit a great deal from working on the representational quality of language and its particular origins in the sense of the body. It also has a very interesting task that psychoanalysts would benefit tremendously from: how does the infant and the child assimilate the grammar of their mother tongue before learning the language and its usage. Peculiarly, Politzer, a philosopher, predicted almost ninety years ago that psychoanalysis was just the beginning, predicting its place in the future endeavors to defining the human subject (1994/1928).

NOTES

1. The Euclidian model of the rotation of the planets in our solar system was informative and in hindsight would classify as idiographic, although it was not dealing with a cultural issue. The Copernicus–Kepler heliocentric model remained an idiographic piece of information until Newton deduced from it the laws of gravity. Thence, the heliocentric model became the prototype of all-star constellations in the universe and the pioneering nomothetic theory of astronomy.

2. Experiments are meant to compare a fixed and controlled condition with identical but uncontrolled conditions. They are meant to answer questions about causes because their design varies the conditions that could create the phenomenon. Thus,

the effect of changing some variable of the condition could lead to explaining the phenomenon. There are no controllable (fixed) conditions in psychoanalysis that could be studied experimentally, as there is no experimental design that would fit the uncontrollable conditions of psychoanalytic material.

3. Analysts derive a sense of distinction from calling themselves psychoanalysts. As clinicians they used to be the first officially trained practitioners in an identified method of treatment. However, training in psychotherapy is no longer a monopoly of psychoanalysis, besides the fact that psychoanalysis has suffered over the years from varying degrees of deterioration all over the world. Thus, even if we restrict psychoanalysis to its clinical field, it is no longer enough to justify the narcissism gained from calling themselves something that were not, or at least no longer are. The psychoanalytic institutions are not anymore the place were psychoanalysis thrives, because clinical psychoanalysis is in dire times, and its informative theory has reached its limit.

4. The "other" is vital in the development of any self-concept because a child starts life without a sense of self and gets it from his relationship with the mother. The success or failure in establishing a stable sense of self would make the other vital in the person's sense being.

5. Persona is the mask actors in the ancient theater of Greece used to personify the character they were playing: Jupiter, Athena, an ordinary citizen, etc. The term was used later as one of three classes of pronouns and as a synonym of the individual in his bodily state. However, a person is what the individual represents to others as a presence.

6. The transformation of somato-affective stimulation into mental and psychical material with the psychological being in a state of precociousness and unconsciousness is the constituent that builds the subject; the dynamic nature of that process becomes the fabric of the "intrapsychic" core of that subject. Some analysts would say that this theory is physicalistic and not psychological. However, what else is the subject but his living body? If he is not his body what could be the origin of the psychical life of the subject? The psychical, of humans in particular, is a chain of transformations that springs from the body, but never ceases to produce new transformations, i.e., transformations of transformation, except when a point of fixation is created during development, and the production of transformation changes into a compulsion to repeat the fixated transformation.

SIX

Future Psychoanalysis

Politics and Organization

There is little disagreement between psychoanalysts of all theoretical backgrounds on the current uncertain state of psychoanalysis. In the previous chapters I discussed briefly the evolution and changes in the attitudes toward that crisis. It appears that over the years psychoanalysts were gradually realizing that they were unable to solve that crisis on their own, and they needed the support and help of other disciplines. At the beginning they did that reluctantly and with a sense of entitlement to get that help from the other branches of the humanities. They needed their "scientific" means to give psychoanalysis back its lost credibility. When this call did not get the expected response, psychoanalysts stepped out of their clinical isolation and showed some modesty. Freedman said (1974): "I foresee dramatic changes taking place in the practice of psychoanalysis because . . . Freud's own prediction will come to pass: that the future will probably attribute far greater importance to psychoanalysis as a science of the unconscious than as a therapeutic procedure" (40). His conclusion talked more about a gloomy future for the profession of psychoanalysis because of the shrinking need for its participation in the clinical field in general. Royden and Astley (1974) made a very concise and precise assessment of the situation by saying:

> Despite Freud's conviction that the great contributions of psychoanalysis would not be found in its therapeutic endeavors, but rather in what it can offer in terms of child-rearing, education, continuing research, the broadening and deepening of the social sciences and the humanities, and its applications in medical and cultural areas—despite that conviction, the education and the activities of psychoanalysts have continued largely to embrace therapeutic competence as though it were

> enough. We have, it is true, made significant beginnings at extending our knowledge and skills and at enlarging our experience beyond the classical, basic, and indispensable therapeutic dyad. For the most part, however, we do not invest much energy or time outside three areas: psychoanalytic practice, teaching and consultation, and the education and training of candidates in our institutes. . . . Perhaps this tendency toward polarization of the therapists on the one hand, and of those, on the other, who wish to apply psychoanalysis to education, child-rearing, and prevention, is a reflection—I use the word again—of ignorance. (84)

The clarity of the situation in the minds of many psychoanalysts, exemplified in those two quotations, made some more daring analysts go ahead and suggest opening psychoanalysis to the wide world of the humanities.[1] Bornstein (2001), in a very astute paper on "the pending death of psychoanalysis," puts the blame squarely on the psychoanalysts. He identifies seven alienating stands they take, which distance psychoanalysis from the rest of the humanities, and suggest three scenarios for the future of psychoanalysis: (1) Some psychoanalytically trained or oriented psychologists will start a wave of researching psychoanalytic issues. He did not have much hope for that scenario. (2) Let it die and donate its parts to other human sciences to keep it viable and to vitalize others, but again did not specify those parts. (3) Let it die and pray for possible future resurrection. Bornstein, in his semi-sarcastic paper, has his hand on the pulse: either psychoanalysis will revitalize other sciences that are also dealing with the human subject but have less means to define it properly, or it will emerge in the future after the other idiographic sciences succeed in studying the human subject well, thus will put psychoanalysis back on the map.

Bucci, as a psychologist, which makes her a cognitive scientist besides her psychoanalytic training, looked at both sides of the situation: the contributions of psychoanalysis to the cognitive sciences, and psychoanalysis's need for cognitive sciences. She says (2000): "Cognitive science has incorporated seminal concepts of psychoanalysis without acknowledging this influence" (203). After showing some of the shortcomings of the subdivision in academic psychology, she argued that "scientific psychology requires a subfield of psychoanalytic psychology that covers the integration of information processing functions, including somatic and emotional processes, in the context of an individual's overall goals. Such a science (psychoanalysis) needs to draw on related fields such as developmental psychology, cognitive psychology, psycho-linguistics, and neuropsychology—and in return has much to offer them" (Ibid., 221–22). Bucci takes the position that the way out of the crisis is the cooperation of both sides. In spite of her strong argument she did not give convincing reasons for the cognitive sciences' need or desire to cooperate in order to save psychoanalysis from its fate. Therefore, her suggestion looks more like the outcome of the solution than the means to it. We should not ignore that psychoanalysts were initially the reluctant party in cooperating and were satisfied with the occasional findings in the other fields that supported their claims. At the same time, psychoanalysts did not come with any major idea that could be reformulated to become a subject of research in the other fields of the humanities.

Eisold is also of Bucci's opinion that a cooperative effort is necessary to give the dying psychoanalysis a future. He said (2003):

> Earlier, in 1916, it [psychoanalysis] had been a "movement," earlier still a "cause." But gradually over the years it seemed to achieve the status for which it had slowly and inexorably striven. That is, like other professions, it possessed an esoteric and specialized body of knowledge, which it sought to develop and extend through journals, books, and conferences; it established institutes to train practitioners in the skillful use of that knowledge; it monitored standards of competence through professional associations; and it developed standards of ethical practice. As a result, psychoanalysts were coming to have a certain recognizable social identity and, like other professionals, lay claim to a corresponding social status.
>
> The professionalization of psychoanalysis in this period paralleled the development of other professions out of relatively unorganized, unregulated, and vulnerable vocations. Social theorists in the earlier part of the century, such as Weber and Durkheim, essentially agreed with the profession's own self-assessment as self-regulating and stable occupations occupying a unique, privileged social position. For them, the idealized position of the professions stemmed in large part from the idea that professions took responsibility for their own development and practice, providing an alternative to the unbridled competition of the marketplace. No doubt, it was this idealized concept of the professions that Freud had in mind when he staked the claim of psychoanalysis. (575–76)

Eisold—differing with Bornstein—(mentioned above) believes in the inevitability of progressing toward a future psychoanalysis that will be a cooperation of several disciplines in the humanities. Bucci's and Eisold's arguments touch a main thought unarticulated stumbling block in the way of future psychoanalysis: *the narcissistic gain analysts derive from their identity of psychoanalysts.* I mean by narcissism in this context, some unjustified and unsubstantiated over valuation of a non-personal and subjective identity that is completely founded on alienation. Future psychoanalysis, as portrayed in those arguments and others similar in essence, would not take place unless the false narcissism derived from a past sense of distinction is abandoned, and replaced with true narcissism founded on new distinguished cooperative work with equally distinguished professionals.

But why would—or should—there be psychoanalysis in the future? Isn't that in itself a narcissistic belief or claim?

Psychoanalysis started with clinical work with a few neurotic patients. New ideas were gathered on the nature of the psychoneuroses. Hypnotism changed into a means to reveal those unconscious impulses that are behind the symptoms of other patients. The repressed proved to be able to speak for itself despite its repression, thus hypnosis was abandoned and listening to the different ways the repressed talks gave birth to more aspects of the psychoneuroses. A dialectical relationship between theorizing and practice was firmly established. However, that relationship proved to be unique: psychoanalysis was a discovery of the nature of the individual whose existence was based on several dialectical psychical dynamics. Better, the individual is in a dialectical state of existence because his "person" is constantly trying to keep balance of conflicting attributes; seldom does he reach that balance but never ceases to keep trying. The theory of psychoanalysis was a treasure trove of information about those states of imbalance. The classical informative theory revealed the nature of the individual, which was a puzzle to humanity in general, and was a breakthrough to the different and varied attempts at understanding him by philosophers, clergymen, physiologists, and a number of other branches of science. However, the classical theory now reached a junction where it could either perish because it has no more information to reveal, or reach for its structural base to look at the individual as a subject, thus gets reborn anew. The structural base is not about the individual but about the human subject, who is more than the balance and imbalance of conflicting attributes. Present human and idiographic sciences are grappling with phenomena like consciousness, the mind and the linguistic foundation of thinking, social structures and human evolution, historical determinism, and even the underlying processes of international and global dynamics. These topics and many similar ones are not explainable by the psychology or the phenomenology of the individual but are indicators of a more complex being. However, although the idiographic sciences have been more focused than at any time before on the concept of the human subject, especially in the fields of language and sociology, they still do not have a firm grasp of its psychological nature. Psychoanalysis in its tradition of the dialectical relationship between theory and practice could and should keep its pioneering and important function in the study of the human subject. Future psychoanalysts, clinical and non-clinical, would be able to give some answers to other sciences' questions, but more importantly provide them with the pertinent questions that could make them advance their endeavors. This is why there should be and will be future psychoanalysis.

Psychoanalysts are able to provide valuable observations on puzzling issues about the nature of the attributes of the subject, their transformations in the process of development, the experiences that create the individuality of the subject, and more about the links between childhood and psychopathology. The psychoanalyst sees the human subject from the best distance which would allow making detailed analysis of his observations. The human subject that we have the advantage of witnessing in treatment engages the analyst in a relationship which reactivates the previous formative relationships (transference). The analyst has the advantage of witnessing those experiences, observes the resistance to change, and the changes happening when analysis works well. The analyst's participation in the future studying of the human subject will give him a place in a community of scientists and thinkers who will be building and maybe practicing a new theory of the human subject. Such theory will not only be a substitute for the present partial one, but it will also be built on the foundations of Freud's method of thinking, because the psychoanalytical theory that will be used is the structural form of the classical theory. Therefore, any psychological notions of the human subject will still be psychoanalytical or a psychoanalysis.

PSYCHOANALYSIS OF THE FUTURE

Analysts do not accept well—or at all—that they have reached the limits of their understanding of the individual, and that there are still unexplainable attributes of the individual that should be explained by non-analysts. For example: we encounter in the transference phenomenon a strong pressure to stop the process of interpretation and a demand to gratify the precocious desire. We know that this is a repetition of the modality of the patient-child relationship. Yet, the repetition is never exactly the same, because what the patient expects from the analysts is not the same as what he wanted to get from the mother. What is repeated is the structure of the demand and the demand itself. More importantly, if the analyst gratifies the patient's desire the problem gets very complicated (like sexual indiscretion with the patient). We do not know though how the childhood desire is structured to be impossible to gratify, or if gratified it conflicts with other aspects of the patient's psychical life. Another example: we know little about the child acquiring and assimilating the grammar of his mother's tongue before mastering language. This fact in child development and the function of language have a very significant place in knowing how psychoanalysis works, because we would hope that the patient learns from his analysis the grammar of its new language, and not only its vocabulary. So after termination he could apply the grammar to understand himself. I have in mind four child psychologist "of my time" who came up with fascinating research about the formation of ideas and thought processes (Vygotsky and Kozalin of Russia), the structuring of the intrapsychic cognitive structures (Piaget of Switzerland), and the emergence of the sense of identity (Wallon of

France). If we think of what a Vygotsikian and a Piagetian could do with questions like: How does a child discover irony and what does his laughter really reflect the intrapsychic structure, we will be close to learning the secrets of the workings of the primary process. Child psychology was interested in psychoanalysis years ago and was revived in the 1960s, but it faded away Demos (1985) said: "Over the last two decades a vast increase in research findings about infants has yielded an astonishing amount of new information. It is not an exaggeration to say that we are currently witnessing a revolution in our thinking about the infant's capabilities and the developmental process. And, as in all revolutions, older established theories are likely to be radically altered or discarded. In this particular revolution, the two theories most vulnerable to challenges are the developmental theories proposed by psychoanalysis and by Piaget. Psychoanalysts have become increasingly interested in the findings from infant research and are asking whether and in what ways their clinical work and theoretical assumptions must be affected. Joseph Lichtenberg's book *Psychoanalysis and Infant Research* is just such an inquiry" (552).

I am thinking of something we analysts need to know more about, as Stechler ask this question (1985): "What does recently acquired body of data from infant research have to say about specific propositions within psychoanalysis; what are the points of compatibility and incompatibility?" (531). An infant of a few months is able to laugh, giggle, and seems to be able to notice ironies in simple situations. Laughing seems to come easier in young age than in older age. We would benefit from knowing how children see irony (or what do they laugh at or about), because we need to know what is a better way of posting an interpretation to a patient. An interpretation is the uncovering of some irony in what the patient thinks, feels, or does and is subtly forming his complaint and character. An example is in order: A friend was telling me about a dream he had of being in heaven and God was giving instructions to kill him. He was laughing his head off in the dream while watching the preparations for his murder. He finished telling me the dream by saying he does not remember the last time he laughed as he laughed in the dream. I asked of what he was laughing about. He stopped for a moment to think and said: "maybe because if I am in heaven I must be dead already, or do you think I was hiding my fear of death!!!" I doubt that there are many analysts who know much about laughing. Even Freud's remarkable book on jokes (1905) does not tell us much about why the discovery of ironies amuses us that mush (he mentioned something about the release of the super ego's control, but nothing about the way the mind grasps irony in a joke).

Curiously, both the present generation of psychoanalysts and the contemporary thinkers got stuck in their examination of *the subject of the human subject*. Present-day analysts are disputing what to consider essential in psychoanalysis, particularly what is the main issue in clinical work.

There is a new generation of patients with psychical disorders (as psychoneuroses have vanished). Analysts have almost nothing to contribute to understanding the new pathological conditions. Their writings are marked by changing old terminologies into new improvised ones (acting out changed to enactment) thinking that they advance the theory by doing that. At this point it is important to emphasize and accentuate a difference between a theory of the subject and its place in future psychoanalysis and the new popular "intersubjective-systems theory." Intersubjectivity as Stolorow stipulates considers (2011): "psychoanalysis is neither a branch of medicine nor of psychology; it is applied philosophy" (12). Yet his and his collaborators' point of departure is traditional psychoanalysis, and their affiliation is to the psychoanalytic establishment, and their official stance is discrediting the theory of psychoanalysis with the declared intention of replacing it. Therefore, we should examine the place of intersubjectivity in future psychoanalysis despite their author's rejection of belonging to it.

Stolorow states that intersubjectivity rejects the notion of the intrapsychic in favor of the idea that "all forms of unconsciousness are constituted in relational contexts." It is implicit in this statement—and others (2012) which are against the existence of any psychical event prior to being experienced within an intersubjective encounter—to conclude that unconsciousness is a creation of relationships and not the initiator of relationships. There is always a problem with issues of cause and effect because reversing them does not change the relationship in a major way. The problem is that the classical theory has said the same thing about some other axioms of the intersubjectivity, but from the opposite end of the argument the intrapsychic is the source and the active originator of interpersonal relationships. As the statement implies, intersubjectivity is not theory of the subject but an elaboration of the phenomenon of subjectivity (vs. objectivity) founded on blatant misunderstanding of Freud's text, and substandard understanding of phenomenological and existential philosophies.[2]

Psychoanalysts are more aware and accepting that there is no termination of any analysis, successful or unsuccessful, and have no convincing explanation of that in a psychoanalytic framework. Clinical analysts are aware of their limitations but instead of looking at what they are analyzing and if it is possible to eradicate it, they turn the ineptness into frustration with the theory. For instance, an average psychoanalyst nowadays is not trained to treat a generation of patients who were brought up by parents who absorbed unconsciously many psychoanalytic ideas. In the 1950s and until the early 1970s the old nosology of psychoneuroses was still applicable with some additional sophistication, like differentiating between psychosomatic disorders and conversion hysteria, or the narcissistic character disorder and the borderline conditions. Gradually the diagnosis of character disorders (e.g., narcissistic personality, passive aggressiveness) took over from the psychoneuroses of the hysterias and the obsessions, which looks as if they have disappeared from the psychoanalytic psychopathology and from the psychoanalytic lexicon. The old psychodynamic conceptions do not have the same explanatory success which the classical theory had with the traditional psychoneuroses, neither do the new object-relations approach or intersubjectivity have any explanations to psychopathology in general, let alone the new ones (Green 2000).

Not only psychoanalysts lost their bearings; contemporary thinkers are also stuck. In contrast with psychoanalysts, they rightly think and discuss what is natural and normal in the human subject. Freud was clear that psychoanalysis should primarily be a theory of the normal. However, psychoanalysis was the culprit in discovering the non-existence of such thing as "normal" or normality. If there is no criterion for normality and at the same time the subject is not the individual who becomes sick, thinkers and other human scientists would be studying a very intriguing subject. The approach to the nature of the human subject confronts the thinker with the phenomenon of consciousness, and its antithesis of aconsciousness (Fayek 2014). The human subject is only *there* in his consciousness; if he exists he will only be a phenomenon of his consciousness. What does it mean that "I am conscious"? The problem with consciousness, which still has no explanation, is the role of the unconscious in instigating it, because all the studies show that there is a substantial input in conscious processes from other mental processes that are out of the range of consciousness (see Fayek 2014). The familiar meaning of the unconscious in the psychoanalytic theory as *the repressed* does not make sense to the thinkers, off course. They do not see how repressed consciousness could create unrepressed consciousness (Freud 1923b). Neurologists too recognized and appreciated the significance of the mental processes that precede consciousness and play a vital role in initiating consciousness, but they could not find what they were looking for in the concept of the repressed. Thinkers and neurologists too are getting frustrated because psychoanalysis raised the issue of the existence of unconsciousness but did not come up with a useful explanation of what it is.

By now, we come to realize a few things. Clinical psychoanalysis has reached the point where it has to change, because analysts have used up the potentials of the informative theory. The outcome of practice is less than satisfactory because analysts are analyzing the individual without good knowledge of the psychology of the subject. Thinkers are not looking for current psychoanalysis to explain the human subject. Notwithstanding, Freud's *implicit* structural theory put some of the individual's intrinsic attributes in focus and for the first time and in an inviting way to rethink both the theory of psychoanalysis and its links with a whole gamut of ideographic sciences. The human subject does not always react in comprehensible ways to stimulations, indicating that a lot of mental activity happens in the time between stimulation and reaction. For instance, humans do not drink when their hydration is close to depletion like other animals do; they feel thirsty and desiring of certain liquids first. Psychoanalysis showed that feeling thirsty could generate a wide range of emotional, psychical, and mental reactions. Moreover, it is very common that certain emotional conditions that have nothing to do with hunger—such as anxiety—could give the person a sense of thirst that is not related to a need or the replenishment of lost hydration. The human subject is the only primate that from his birth his somatic needs generate representations of those needs, such as in sucking his thumb. The representations become the social medium that humans use in their interaction (when that fails the animal in us breaks through our human quality). Representations are the foundation of language because they are ideational and communicable; hence language becomes an action in its own right. This array of human characteristics takes psychoanalysis to the limits of its capability. Analysts know nothing about the transformation of physical need into a mental activity which emerges and evolve into a characteristic of the human infant. They also know little about the attainment of the linguistic faculty. A clinical analyst *needs* to know those things to be able to understand his patient's expression of himself and to know how to formulate his interpretations.

Thinkers, child psychologists, linguists, and sociologists have and could have more information about those aspects especially if they knew their significance in studying the human subject. Psychoanalysts are in a position to raise those questions and put the results in a proper perspective. It is imperative at this point to point out two things. We struggle with the transformations of the physiological into psychological, psychological into mental, the mental into the personal, and that into unique subjectivities. We deal in our practice with aspects of subjectivity and personal preferences that we know nothing about, or very little. We could also raise the problem of the infant's brain and its functioning. Basch (1985) said: "What we think we see retrospectively in our work with our patients is dependent upon our preoccupation whether articulated or not, about development" (514). Does the infant's brain function differently from the adult brain? Or is it a matter of maturation? This is a central problem in clinical psychoanalysis because clinically we deal with fixations on childish ways of thinking, reacting, and inabilities in differentiating between past and present, etc. This issue raises a string of questions about the core propositions of psychoanalysis regarding development, transformation, interpretation, and construction and reconstruction. We know from Piaget that children from age five develop a sense of right or wrong which looks like a moral code. If that is true, is adult morality a development of that childhood quasi-sense of morality, is morality an adulthood attainment or a childhood achievement? With little speculation we can envisage that a new psychoanalysis based on the psychology of the subject would be truly different from the present dwindling one. Our understanding of patients would change if the aforementioned aspects, and more aspects of the same kind, are clarified to us by the researchers, thinkers, and professionals in those fields of knowledge. Future psychoanalysis will derive a substantial part of its new structural theory from being part of a wide circle of sciences, and part of a host of human sciences that are dedicated to the study of the subject. Clinical psychoanalysis will not be an isolated pseudo-professional endeavor of no convincing theory supporting it, or of a therapeutic outcome that verifies it; it will become an important part of the burgeoning interest in the human subject.

Freud talked about future psychoanalysis saying (1926e): "Analytic instructions [in the future] would include branches of knowledge which are remote from medicine and which the doctor does not come across in his practice: the history of civilization, mythology, the psychology of religion, and the science of literature. Unless he is well at home in these subjects, the analysts can make nothing of a large amount of his material" (246). Freud was aware that clinical psychoanalysis is limited and learning it as a mental health profession is more than just unfavorable; it is harmful. Although he is not suggesting a radical change in psychoanalytic training he is clearly saying "a psychoanalyst has to be cultured." However, human sciences have advanced and expanded to a degree that whatever the analyst tries to learn would not be enough. Psychoanalysts will always need the scientists of those sciences to be active participants and direct sources of information for them. Psychoanalysts should realize their lack of basic facts about the psychological, mental, social, and neurological structuring of the human subject. They should see that their future requires, if not demands, that they become part of the integrated efforts of the scientists of the humanities and the thinkers of metaphysics. This obvious new situation makes the psychoanalysts face two duties: (1) To know enough of the subjects of the other sciences to be able to form intelligent questions to ask (2) and make the scientists of those sciences know and understand something about the psychoanalytical issues that preoccupy them. A future cultured analyst has to be well conversed in those new fields of knowledge to link properly with them.

There is a feature in the possible link between future psychoanalysis and the other related sciences that could change—in a significant way—the nature of scientific activities. Up until now, each specialty has its scientific gatherings and organizations. If they are to eventually cooperate they must develop a system to get them together, hopefully regularly, to educate each other about their work. Greek philosophy was the project of getting all the proper questions out of the bag that they left for Western philosophers to examine. Their philosophical endeavors paved the way for the nomothetic sciences to ultimately emerge. Psychoanalysis could assume the same function by becoming the project that reveals the inadequacies of studying the individual outside his whole subjective background, thus make the psychology of the subject a demanding issue that needs to be met. In order to do that, psychoanalysts have to change their attitude. They should not open their organizations to non-analytic specialists (as it is happening now in some societies) because it is in the first place an implicit message of superiority. Second, it will not encourage too many to attend or commit for too long because the psychoanalytic meetings are usually clinically oriented. *Psychoanalysts should seek the meeting of the other branches of the humanities and train themselves to listen to non-clinical presentations.* It will not be easy to achieve that at the beginning but psychologists—psychoanalysts—have much better chance than the non-psychologists. The psychological societies and associations all over the world have, at least, sections for more than one specialty within psychology. This would be the first step toward opening up to other specialties, because psychologists in those specialties are usually linked with the related branches of the humanities that are close to them. Thus, psychoanalysts would take those links within their associations as spring boards to spread their wings. If psychoanalysts connected well with non-analysts and established common ground between them it would not be difficult to form organizations for the psychoanalytically inclined people irrespective of their training. Once again, the Greek model is useful in envisaging the formations of symposia on the Socratic model or academia on the Platonic pattern to exchange knowledge and ideas about the human subject, in which future psychoanalysis becomes one of its contributors.

The changing function of clinical psychoanalysis in future psychoanalysis will change the identity of the analyst. The psychoanalyst as the distinguished psychiatrist, psychologist, social worker, or any other health provider who is trained in psychoanalysis would gradually lose the glitter of the title. The psychoanalytic organization where psychoanalysis will be discussed and disseminated is going to comprise members of very different specialties and the health providers will be only part of it. This does not mean that the present organization of psychoanalysis has to disappear. However, most likely it will eventually dissipate, because it will not be where the seriously interested psychoanalyst finds what meets his expectations, and the less serious ones would not be keen to know more about something they do not consider important.

THE IDENTITY OF THE PSYCHOANALYSTS IN FUTURE PSYCHOANALYSIS

In the 1970s there was a belief that by just tinkering with some aspects of the theory it could be improved. When those attempts failed, the trend in the 1980s went as far as searching for replacements of the whole premise of the classical theory with another.[3] This trend, with its obvious failure to improve the "faulty" theory, took a turn lately thinking that making changes in training modalities and revising the curricula in the institutes might be the right way to save psychoanalysis. There is no doubt that there is a need to do more revisions and update the training modalities, but we should not forget that the deteriorating state of analysis preceded any deteriorations of training. Psychoanalysis is deteriorating because after a hundred years of making minor and major changes here or there in the theory of the individual, or what Ernest Jones called a theory of the mind, we reached the final limitations of an exhausted theory, and we are aimlessly trying to advance the same theory (recycling old concepts and ideas). There is nothing in the current innovations in psychoanalysis that addresses three problems, which all analysts face and have no way or ideas to solve them: (1) We never achieve in psychoanalytic work the theoretical modality of cure (analysis is always an unaccomplished endeavor) or have no technical modality that guides us in our clinical work. (2) We are not learning anything new from our patients who do not fit the psychodynamics of traditional psychoneuroses. (3) The new psychopathologies reveal to the perceptive analysts that he is missing major information about the formation of the human subject in the early years of his life. In a sweeping statement: *We reached the point where we know that we do not know many fundamental things about our subjects, sick or healthy, or how to find them out.*

In 1995, the IPA formed a committee from different societies in different parts of the world to examine "The True Crisis of Psychoanalysis" (Cesio 1995). The crisis still exists and has gotten worse over the last twenty years. It reached the stage of afflicting anything that is called psychoanalysis. It does not take much to realize that without a solid and clear theory of psychoanalysis it is doomed to collapse. Yet, the greatest and main concerns in the organizations of psychoanalysis are the bylaws and training, which were not the causes of the crisis or are going to save psychoanalysis from impending oblivion. In one of the most powerful and prestigious psychoanalytic organizations (reported in the newsletter of its association) the president of the organization admitted that psychoanalysis is in trouble. He alluded to the real threat of the declining number of patients who seek psychoanalysis and the young professionals who seek training in analysis. He was asked if we (the analytic association) could still thrive. His answer was yes . . . if the association solves the problem of the training analyst! It is incredible to think that patients and young professionals lack an interest in psychoanalysis because there are disagreements about the status of training analysis, and will develop interest in psychoanalysis when the "organization" will solve the problem of accrediting the training analysts. The answer to the question was not about the future of psychoanalysis but the future of the organization of the psychoanalysts.

A serious and honest effort to revive the core propositions of psychoanalysis and to properly articulate its structural theory would not interest today's psychoanalysts. Most of them are settled contently in the title of psychoanalyst and neither do they want to lose it nor do they know how to revive the theory. The luring image of the psychoanalyst is until what it was in the mid-1960s. The analyst was a fascinating person who was supposed to know unusual things about the individual, distinguished by his imposing maturity and psychological health,[4] highly regarded, always the head of any team he worked with, the final word in clinical matters, etc. Fortunately—in my opinion—this is not the current image of the psychoanalyst, and should not be anymore the aspired for image, because psychoanalysis has a more serious task ahead, which does not go with this narcissistic image. Future psychoanalysis is not going to be about the analyst anymore but about psychoanalysis. The main concern all along—from the end of the secret committee—was psychoanalysis as a distinct profession and the analyst as the privileged professional. In other terms, analysts derive a great part of their narcissistic importance from just being analysts and overlooked the fact that psychoanalysis is not anymore the morning star of the humanities. With that background in mind, I would answer the question mentioned above: it is time to move to something else than what was considered psychoanalyses in the last four decades because no one can *firmly* say which psychoanalysis of the last forty years is *the* psychoanalysis one belongs to. But how do we go about the direction we should take to move on?

There is always a hint in the past that suggests what the future should be like. Freud left us with two problems, which his attempts at solving complicated matters further. By the mid-1920s psychoanalysis was a stale theory of the individual in which everything dynamic in the individual was calcified and became mechanical, and the individual was reified in an unmanageable way. The patient treated was, for instance, a creature made of defense mechanisms. It was a theory that would come with statements like: "We try to strengthen the patient's weak ego to face up to an id that is burdened by a harsh super ego." A very informative statement of what we and the patient should spend years talking about! However, in *Inhibitions, Symptoms and Anxiety* (Freud 1926d) Freud infused life in the subject by leaving the individual and his mind aside and presented a new understanding of anxiety: instead of being the result of the pressure of the id it was the state of affect that engenders symptom formation. Yet Freud's revision resulted in a problem: if anxiety instigates the process of symptom formation, then what instigates anxiety? The typical answer to that question at the time was the threat of the instincts. But that would put us in a logical loop: What creates the ego that gets anxious and develops the symptoms that create the anxiety that are dealt with by symptom formation? Freud tried to answer this question in 1937 in *Analysis Terminable and Interminable* and he made a mess of the subject. He configured a model of interplay of forces and valences of those forces that happen in the process of treatment. But he had to concede the fact that psychoanalysis is limited in its therapeutic results. To explain (justify) that limitation he was forced to come up with two unanalyzable bedrock issues: *castration anxiety* and *penis envy*. This means that we have an objective to reach in psychoanalysis but we do not know how to reach it. This is not just an issue of curiosities. The literature is void of any viable answer to it except suggesting models of equally theoretical nature. This is a serious issue because what we only have is a theory of the mind, while the patient is a subject not just a mind. At the same time we know almost nothing about how his mind is structured to work in the way we witness in analyzing him. We need to know how his *Triebhaft* vicissitudes generate their representations. We should accept leaving behind a glorious theory that has served its purpose and move toward another theory about another subject matter. That means taking the uniform off the clinical psychoanalysts and joining the ordinary citizens of the idiographic sciences.[5]

TRAINING AND THE FORMATION OF PSYCHOANALYSTS

Training in psychoanalysis went through many changes over the years and was always a bone of contention and problematic. However it is a requirement only if the person wanted to join the exclusive community of psychoanalysts. Otherwise, any professional who has a license to treat a patient could practice or claim to practice psychoanalysis. If training is the means to acquire the knowledge and the "know-how" of doing analysis, this could be done outside the institutes, and sometimes it would be of better quality than what institutes provide. The three elements of training: personal analysis, seminars, and supervised practice are available out of the reach of the implicit and sometimes explicit politics of the training organizations. Strangely, the debates and conflicts between training analysts and the training committees in most institutes is a known real problem because it is mostly on matters of political nature and seldom related to training or the formation of the candidates. Training analysts on both sides of the fence of the training committees are critical of the standardized and prescribed methods of training, but do nothing active about their dissatisfactions with what they supposedly advocate. This might sound paradoxical, i.e., the ones who do the training are not happy with it, yet they continue doing it. This is clear in the case of the maverick French analyst Jack Lacan. He tried to be consistent with himself and follow his own criticality, but he faced intrinsic problems and expulsion from the IPA for attempting to challenge the organizational model established by Eitington in 1922.[6] His attempt to liberate training from the confines of the institution collapsed and almost brought down the whole Lacanian cause for seemingly a very intriguing and interesting reason: training and the institute are not in the service of psychoanalysis; they are essential for the continued existence of the institution of psychoanalysis. However, it revealed something no one but a Lacan could have exposed. Neither the traditional model of training, nor doing away with it is the solution to the undeniable shortcomings of the current training system of psychoanalysis. Training analysis seems to have a function that is not clear in its declared purpose. How could that be? The problem is not the inadequacy of the training model or the lack of a replacement for it. The problem is in the nature of psychoanalysis itself. Training is supposed to provide the candidate with the theory of analysis and the manner of applying it in practice. In other terms, training is meant to introduce and explain to the candidate the body of knowledge of psychoanalysis (the informative theory) and show him the practice protocols in action in order to make sure that he would know how to apply that information in the manner psychoanalysis requires. However, we know by now that it is the structural theory of psychoanalysis that counts in creating the analytic mind of the analyst and not the landmark concepts or even the basic conceptions of the informative theory. We also know that there are no clinical technicalities in psychoanalysis that could be taught to the candidates, and the whole analytic endeavor is nothing more than free association from the patient and interpretations from the analyst. We do not teach the patient to free associate and we do not teach the candidate how to interpret; it may be possible to teach a child to play the piano but to become *a pianist* is something else. Even though a prodigious pianist would still need a trainer (of a different caliber) he has to have what no teacher could teach, but could only bring out.[7] However, I am not saying that psychoanalysis is an art and some people have the gift for it. What I am saying is that there is a difference between ability and gift. In my opinion and from my experience in training and supervising, training could provide some guidelines and explanations of the protocols of practice, but could only make a good candidate a better analyst. *Training gives the candidate and the training analyst the opportunity to explore together the structural theory of psychoanalysis and to examine the logic of its Freudian practicing protocol.*

Although psychoanalysis was the product of new attempts at making psychotherapy part of medicine, it was claimed early to be a profession in its own right. Working with patients was the only known way—at the time—to carry on the process of discovering the unconscious. Furthermore, psychoanalysis was then and for few more decades just an informative theory, and neither Freud nor the pioneer paid attention to the need for the structural theory. Nevertheless, the discoveries in the nature of the psyche appealed to some non-medical people. The non-medical enthusiasts created a gap in psychoanalytic theory and practice especially that Freud believed from the start until the end that psychoanalysis was more than the practice of analyzing patients. However, as the psychoanalytic circle widened, practicing it as a profession expanded and things were getting out of control. The onset of training was a reaction to the chaotic state of affairs that accompanied the uncontrolled expansion of the psychoanalytic movement in the 1920s, but it was also meant to control the affiliation to the profession. It was thought that by demanding periods of training the analytic community could have an indirect mandate to control the membership to the analytic community. The proof to that is the very elementary and simple training programs adopted at the beginning and Freud exempting some people from it based on his opinion that they did not need it. This proves that training was at the beginning a misnomer because training was not the original objective. However, *the protocol of training and the organizational structure of psychoanalysis of its early years were of unmeasurable significance in maintaining the integrity of the psychoanalytic movement the way it was until the early 1960s.* The institution's adherence to linking training to membership is not to be undervalued. Notwithstanding this fact, we should not ignore the fallacy of maintaining training as a professional requirement when it was only a means to keep some order in the organization from beginning until now.

It is interesting to note that the most recent critiques and dissatisfactions with training are the same from the very beginning of the movement of training. Most of the major difficulties between Freud and some of the early members of his group were about training issues. Founding the training committee 1922 limited the direct conflicts between analysts and their training seniors by creating a political cleavage within the psychoanalytic institution. The psychoanalytic institute canceled the personal factor in the process of training. The cleavage turned training into an impersonal matter and a need that belonged more to the professional obligation not to the candidate's personal benefit or a desire. Making training a requirement to belonging to the psychoanalytic community changed it into an *aspiration,* and we know very well that that aspiration is a facade for a narcissistic demand. Some training analysts witnessed the superficiality of the candidates' dedication to training and the limited results of their personal analysis and raised questions about its effectiveness. Yet, there were no proper answers to several related questions. Limentani answered two of those questions saying (1974): "We must note in passing that the abolition of organized training could only bring in its wake chaotic conditions, including the spreading of 'wild training analyses,' which are already being reported in a number of societies" (73). However, he underlined some major problems with training that are probably so drastic to be openly mentioned. Limentani says (Ibid.): "Institutional training is probably antithetical to analysis" (75). Kernberg has a paper on training titled, "Thirty Methods to Destroy the Creativity of Psychoanalytic Candidates" (1996), which puts in focus the problem of training in today's psychoanalysis. If it is the opinion of the senior analysts that if training is an unavoidable evil why don't they do something about it or suggest something else to replace it? In other words, training analysts are saying that organized training is not only of little worth but sometimes outright counterproductive. But as Limentani remarks: "Such is the nature of the syncretic position in which training analysts and candidate-students have to function, whether they like or not, and irrespective of the measures they take towards limiting it, or eliminating it" (Ibid., 71). The syncretic nature of training must be embedded in something missing in our understanding of psychoanalysis.

The reason for the gradual and predictable unraveling of training is a result of what is missing from our perception of psychoanalysis. Organizing the psychoanalytic institution by enforcing the rule of training was a function of an informative theory that was thriving but evolving in a disorderly manner. Therefore, if the expansion of the theory was to get organized or, as we will see, ceases to happen, the natural outcome is that training will show all the signs we mentioned above: ineffectiveness, becoming a harmful professional requirement, merely a formality to gain recognition, counterproductive in selecting the best to be trained, e.g., it would mostly be supporting narcissistic incentives. Psychoanalysis as informative theory reached a point when it has to undergo changes to assimilate the fruits of its success. At this point all the information it comprised lost value but gave birth to a structural theory of the outdated one. The evolution of the theory of evolution succeeded in assimilating its successes, as it led to discovering the world of genetics. In psychoanalysis we are stuck at the point of knowing only what we know about the individual and we are not advancing to discovering the human subject.

Psychoanalysis, even in its present crisis, has a theory of the human subject in its core, whether we like it or not. Its past is the beginning of the journey humanity took from self-consciousness to psychoanalytic discovery, then to finding out the psyche and its intra-structures. Therefore a brief account of that journey is important to direct our route to future psychoanalysis. In better terms, tens of thousands of years ago *Homo sapiens* developed enough to engender a sense of self. They kept puzzling about its nature and made major discoveries in that regard. Three thousand years ago Thales, a Greek thinker, asked a simple question: How can I be sure of the correctness of what I hear? And logic was born and soon after philosophy came about. Cultures and civilizations before the Greeks posed questions that pertained to matters of impersonal nature; they were mostly about nature and our place in it. Nature was something to explore so humans would live within it as successfully as possible. The Acadian civilization followed by the Sumerian civilization managed to domesticate some animals and some plants allowing humans to be free from the task of gathering food on daily basis. The result of saving energy and time was vital for organizing social life.[8] The civilizations that followed (Assyrian, Babylonian, and Egyptian) were the originators of writing, architecture, social and civil order, the concept of the state, and most of all organized religion. By the time the Greeks came on the scene of the humanities the inhabited world was divided by states, nations, languages, and religion. Religion was a serious and clear indication of the direction that self-consciousness had taken and will take for millennia to come. Central in all religions is how man has begun and how will he end, i.e., what is life about. The questions religion has proposed were closer to the nature of the human being, however, this matter needed thinkers to pose the proper questions.

Greek philosophy started with the human mind. It was the first civilization that raised questions of personal nature about the human mind. Its endeavors mainly took place in symposia or academia where open discussion among the interested and knowledgeable showed the seriousness of philosophy and the true philosophers. Whether some valuable answers came out those efforts or not is dwarfed in comparison with the success of putting the human mind in perspective and making the human subject a philosophical issue in his own right. After a long phase of social upheaval followed by the birth of the new religion of Christianity and the collapse of the Roman Empire, the human subject became and was made a target of Christian speculations. It seemed that when the Greek enlightenment came to an end religion took the seat of philosophy and man had to be inframed in it. What followed was a vigorous movement to improve on the monastic theological arguing of the Bible, i.e., a scholastic movement that raised the issue of the human mind to another level of importance. Scholasticism, despite its ostensible sterility, systematized the discussions and the environments where the human subject was targeted as the subject matter of philosophy. The people behind those endeavors were educated and educators and established universities devoted a part of its activities to that purpose. Thus, the human mind was turned into the equivalent to mathematics and geometry that were studied in the universities. All that happened without good translations of Greek philosophy. Once that translation became available, modern Western philosophy was initiated and its philosophers latched onto the subject of the human subject. They made thinking about the human mind almost a profession. Yet, whatever the progress in exploring the mind, and thinking about thinking, the human mind needed a theory: a starting point to a direction to be taken. This theory was missing, and major particular components were needed to become the spark that started the fire of Western civilization. The spark was the query about the meaning of noticeable specificities of the known human mind, and what the method of systematically exploring them is, e.g., what is knowing, doubting, being-in-the-world, etc. The great edifice of German idealism and the remarkable systemic understanding of the rules of understanding in England were leaps in the journey toward the nature of the human subject and a theory about him. This part of the journey met an obstacle: all that was debated and investigated looked as if it was manifestations of the subject and not the subject himself, and thinkers were not getting any closer to the subject whatever they did to know him. There was more to the human subject than his doubt, his ways of approaching and appreciating reality, sometimes his strangeness, even his self-reporting, etc. A new start had to be discovered to bypass that obstacle.

The final step in the search for a theory of the mind came when Freud stumbled on an evident fact about the individual. The individual could sometimes avoid knowing about himself, because unnoticeably and unintentionally he expels few things out of his consciousness; he represses parts of himself. Those repressed parts are personal and individual thus the approach had to be the study of the individual and not the subject (the abstract of all the individuals). Freud's contribution to the theory of the mind was not discovering the missed part of the subject, which we could—right away—take for granted that it was the unconscious, because the notion of the unconscious was already stated in German ideology. *Freud's breakthrough was discovering the ways the unconscious uncovers itself.* He showed that the unconscious exists in what is manifest of the mental activity, yet disguised in subtle ways. Freud's psychoanalysis was a major shock to Western thinking, not because it was—as Freud thought—a blow to the narcissism of the human subject, but because it was there in the open, looking us in the eye, yet was finely woven in the obvious and missed.

The early years of the psychoanalytic movement examined and explored this new aspect of the mind, discovered most of its vicissitudes, but most of all psychoanalysis familiarized the world with it, no difference in that between an intellectual or an ordinary person. Training and initiation into the "guild" of psychoanalysis kept Freud's momentum hot and active. But we came to a point where analysts should have realized in the theoretical and the organizational turmoil of the 1950s that psychoanalysis has reached its last stage and had to change. It was obvious then, as it is very obvious now, that psychoanalysts should look for a future enterprise that will require a different modality of training and different type of organization.

There are two major stumbling blocks in the road to future psychoanalysis. The first combines two contradictory points of view. Some analysts—who claim to adhere to the classical theory—consider Freud's theory of the mind the only and primary source of psychoanalysis, past, present, and future. In their own mind classical psychoanalysis has to remain the main body of any future psychoanalysis, even though it has been modified substantially over the years. Thus, the informative theory should be maintained although its information is no longer of the same caliber. The contrary opinion is that Freud's theory has to be replaced with another informative theory that would function as the basis for a new and different psychoanalysis. This way future psychoanalysis would be either Freudian or anti-Freudian but Freud's stamp remains on the letter of acceptance and the letter of rejection all the same. The second obstacle is associating psychoanalysis with the "profession" of psychoanalysis. Therefore, future psychoanalysis has to remain a termed and a defined profession, not merely a theory of the human subject. This has been the myth for the first fifty years of its initiation, remained as unshaken conviction of most psychoanalysts until now, when everything is pointing to the fallacy of both the myth and the conviction. Practicing psychoanalysis was for a while the only activity that could lead to discovering the human psyche. This activity might have built the theory in the past but is not sustainable anymore. The profession of psychoanalysis is also unsustainable because of its poor effectiveness as treatment. This means that psychoanalysts who insist on staying in the same clinical modality of sixty years past will be passenger on a sinking ship.

At this point I would argue that the current training programs approved by the IPA for the accredited institutes are clearly of limited benefit to today's psychoanalysts. In reviewing the four main English language journals[9] in the last thirty years, and the irregular reading of other journals in English, I found a large number of papers on *technique*, but not more than eight papers and reports on *training*. I presume that the same might be the case in the journals of the other languages.[10] It seems that confusing the original purpose of training, which was basically to streamline the process of membership in the psychoanalytic community, and the formation of the candidates, has become a built-in problem in the organization of psychoanalysis as a whole. The reason is that the two objectives are not necessarily related. It is not thinkable to train someone to do something fundamentally personal and spontaneous like psychoanalysis. It is also unlikely for an interested person—as genuinely as he could be—to go through the "tripartite" components of traditional training on his own and independently of the official training modalities.[11] Furthermore, non-officially recognized analysts could and did form their own associations and were quite successful in keeping psychoanalysis the center of attention, but that venue of affiliation to the community of psychoanalysis did not appeal to many. Just as an example of confusing the objectives of training analysis I quote Calef (1972) in summarizing the IPA meeting on training:

> To conclude this report, I take this opportunity to ask some questions. . . . Once the training analysis was considered a modification of therapeutic analysis, and therefore primarily didactic, not therapeutic. The emphasis has gradually changed, so that now it is put on the therapy. Are we not caught in the duplicity and the inconsistency of insisting it is a modification (for training), while we have changed its historical intent by also insisting that it be more and more focused on therapeutic aims, in the hope that the educational aims will simply follow automatically from the therapy? If it is true that we are caught

> up in processes essentially based on erroneous assumptions, defended on humanitarian and educational grounds, as well as on confidentiality and the principle of syncretism leading towards the separation of didactic analysis from the psychoanalytic education, we may face the loss of what may be the unique contribution offered by psychoanalysis to education, namely the consideration of the individual as a unique instrument of learning, with special needs which can only be determined by analysis! . . . Is it not possible that many of the proliferations and the alternatives of our educational methods are attempts to re-establish the unique psychoanalytic contribution to education which cannot be replaced by other didactic means since they cannot serve the same functions? (41–42)

The original purpose of personal analysis was to learn how it was done and was not for therapeutic purposes. It changed to become a therapeutic procedure although we all know that therapeutic analysis has to be independently sought after, not for any other purpose than treatment. We also know that didactic analysis has created internal conflicts in most if not all the psychoanalytic societies due to residual transference and counter transference of the therapeutic procedure. The relationship between the members and the senior members (the training analysis) continues to impact the politics of the society. The transference and counter transference residuals which stay with the candidate after becoming members of the society imbue the political scenes with their biases.

As a reminder of the changes that should and would be the nature of future psychoanalysis I will give a very pertinent quote that brings us back to the impossibility of maintaining psychoanalysis embalmed in the shroud of its professionalism.

Eisold summarized his paper (2003) by saying:

> Freud's definition of psychoanalysis as "a collection of psychological information" led to the establishment of a rigid boundary between psychology and psychoanalysis, which we are only recently coming to dismantle. And his definition of it as a "treatment for neurotic disorders" led to the virtually endless effort to define a boundary with "psychotherapy" in the attempt to sustain a privileged apartness. Loosening those boundaries will inevitably bring psychoanalysis closer to the larger worlds of psychology and psychotherapy, relieving it from the contradictions of its superior aloofness. It will also, I believe, help to clarify its primary mission.
>
> If it were possible to agree on the essential psychoanalytic task of inquiry and exploration, how would that affect the nature of our "professional project?" What would psychoanalysis look like?
>
> For one thing, such psychoanalysis would have to see itself in the context of other professions and disciplines, abandoning its tendency toward isolation and aloofness, its tendency to see itself as uniquely qualified and hierarchically privileged. We would need to work at building links with other fields, demonstrating our willingness and interest in

> collaborating—and, of course, our ability to do so. Collaboration with other disciplines would require extended exposure to allied fields, not merely psychotherapy. Not only would training need to provide a more culturally diverse range of offerings, but suggesting how psychoanalysis could be enriched by and could, in turn, enrich other disciplines. Training would need to include exposure to other clinical areas as well, in larger systems such as groups, families, and organizations, in order to gain some familiarity with complex clinical phenomena. (581–82)

Moving toward future psychoanalysis that becomes part of a larger circle of specialties would put the issue of training in a different perspective. The first perspective is the difference between forming the analytic mind, training and preparing the candidate to be part of that wider circle. Training has to change in its basic objectives personal analysis for therapeutic results, supervision to learn analysis and avoid making the mistakes that spoil the process, and attending theoretical seminars that would include non-analysts and would be taught by non-analysts to learn about the human subject. Most of all, accepting being a member in the psychoanalytic community, locally and internationally, should not be decided by being trained in an accredited institute. The societies are rife with "trained" analysts who contribute nothing to psychoanalysis, while there are non-trained people who contribute to psychoanalysis either by invitation or by natural proclivity to psychoanalytic thinking. There are non-analysts who could enrich the scientific life of the local societies and institutes. In the future, it should be known that going through training in an institute does not guarantee membership to the society, because training is to satisfy an already licensed heath provider with an education to practice psychotherapy in a proper way. Membership in the society could be attained by presenting works in any specialty in the humanities that either follow the principles of the structural theory of psychoanalysis, or contribute to that theory.

Therefore, training programs need to change in orientation if we are to take psychoanalysis out of its slump. First, it should be open to non-clinicians because the objective of training is the formation of the psychoanalytic mentality, and the psychoanalytic way of thinking, not the formation of the professional clinician. Thus, training should not be decided by the time needed to cover basic informative aspect of the literature, or the number of supervised patients or supervisions. Personal analysis should be encouraged but not mandated, and consulting experienced analysts about the treatment of patients should also be a personal choice. The candidate choice of the seminars he wants to attend is a good criterion for joining—officially—the new psychoanalytic organization. A review of the Freudian text and the landmark works of gifted and inspiring analysts are essential in building a syllabus for the seminars. Some of Freud's work links well with those areas of the humanities that should have an equal place in the syllabus. This addition should be taught by people who are specialized in those fields and not by psychoanalysts (I think of the Lacanians who would have benefited more from the rich hints Lacan was sparkling his seminars with, if they were expanded and delivered by specialist in those fields). This way we could avoid what Lacan once said: "the psychoanalytic literature is like Agamemnon's Stables; it needs an Achelous to clean it form the manure that fills it." The point is that membership in the psychoanalytic community should reflect the person's "desire" to learn how to think psychoanalytically and not to just attain the title. We encounter clinical issues and problems that have solutions in other fields of the humanities, but we need to know how to formulate our questions in the terms of the specialty we are in need of its help.

The second perspective is to introduce psychoanalysis to that wider circle of the specialists in the humanities. Future psychoanalysis would or should be in the form of symposia (the Socratic symposium), where a group of similar minds but of different backgrounds gathers regularly to discuss their works. The symposia would eventually lead to the kind of dedicated studies characteristic of the academia (Plato). I can envisage a department of linguistics in the local university organizing and sponsoring a symposium like that, where it gradually involves interested people in the studies of the subjects: psychologist, philosophers, anthropologists, linguists, gifted thinkers, promising students, etc. This perception of future psychoanalysis is not fictional as most contemporary analysts would think. In the 1920s an unofficial symposium like that emerged on an international scale without any formal call for its organization. Thinkers from different ways of life and corners of the world engaged in serious debates about psychoanalytic findings. The literature of psychoanalysis, literature, philosophy, art, politics, etc., was full of works interwoven into a unique psychoanalytic blanket. Psychoanalysts at that time were thinkers and followed the discussions and contributed to it. By the 1950s and to an extent in the 1960s a great number of important theorists, psychologists, philosophers, anthropologists, logicians, linguists, novelists, and playwrights gave psychoanalysis another breath of life, but unfortunately clinical analysts, who monopolized analysis, were more interested in improving the technical aspects of analytic practice. Even Lacan who was the most stimulating analyst by culture and most promising to stimulate culture turned his back to that endeavor after (as it was said) a disappointing meeting with Heidegger. He decided to occupy the whole space and leave little to others. However, there is hope and need for opening up psychoanalysis to be part of a comprehensive theory of the subject.

The participation of psychoanalysts in such symposia requires that they would have the theoretical orientation that turns their clinical problems into non-clinical problems, thus attracting the interest of the non-clinical specialists. For example, in every psychoanalysis we face the problem of the indirect conception of the self, e.g., I said to myself, I think that I am . . . etc. We have to have a good description of what we mean by narcissism to explain that feature in a language that would interest the child psychologists, the linguist (the usage of pronouns), and possibly the neurologist. In order to do that we need to know a few things about those disciplines to be able to put the problem in front of the whole symposium for them to participate in finding answers to our questions. What is the basis of the double sense of being? We also need to learn how to relate their problems to our psychoanalytic findings. Furthermore, we should have in our training programs some seminars that would interest the non-analysts to attend.

There is a firm link between psychoanalysis and its institutions. In spite of the undeniable fragmentation of the theory after Freud's death and the obvious need for giving it all the attention to solve its problems, analysts were more vigorous and hot-headed in disagreeing about their institutions and competing for positions on the governing boards of those institutions. Analysts were more concerned about the organization than what the organization's basic function is: protect psychoanalysis before protecting the psychoanalysts.

THE ORGANIZATION AND INSTITUTION OF FUTURE PSYCHOANALYSIS

Making a distinction between the human subject and the individual who is merely a representation of the subject could be puzzling and difficult, because we actually know next to nothing about the human subject. We have only a vague and sketchy idea about what and how mental processes and their emotional concomitants emerge and get connected in the first three years of life. When we later encounter the *outcome* of such development we give it some abstract meaning like assimilation, or in Kleinian terminology introjection, or identifying with. We refer a great deal of the psychodynamics of interpersonal relations to those "processes." However, those terminologies are assumptions about matters that should be properly observed and documented, then examined by several specialized scientists to provide psychoanalysis with the insights about what is called introjection, etc. Similarly, because language is considered a human endowment and acquiring it is natural we miss some of its foundational aspects, which would be most essential in our clinical work. We know almost nothing about the link between the vocabulary and the grammar in our speech, while learning those links are essential in acquiring a foreign language. The input of the linguist and the neurologist in this point is most important to psychoanalysis because the speech we listen to in analysis is not a learned language but the verbalization of an intrapsychic structure. The speech of the patient and the interpretation of the analyst replicate the relationship the patient had with the mother, not as transference but as an actual attempt at understanding each other through an unconscious medium, language.[12]

Analysts have some speculative ideas about what fascinates the infant when he sees his mother's face, but we also know nothing about the power of the "gaze" in our adult intrapsychic dynamics. We notice that kids understand speech before six months but we do not know when they develop a sense of communicating after being communicated with by the caregivers. This knowledge is important for the analysts. Many a time we realize that our interpretations are going nowhere because the patient seems to be unaware that the interpretation given is communication; he instead carries on with his monologue. We do not know most, if any, of what constructs and builds the neurotic core of the subject, because we lack the idea of how children (of different ages) perceive what is expected of them. In spite of the rich literature on the manifestations of introjection, narcissistic mortification, reaction formation, etc., which become master-keys to understanding the individuals we treat, there is nothing in the literature to explain what made those "mechanisms" turn into a way of living for those patients. Those mechanisms were the child's best way to live his psychical life and were weaved in his adult life in a confusing way. Child psychologists could give us insights in how childhood cognition could form those mechanisms and become the pattern of "understanding the social environment later in adulthood."

In nomothetic sciences every new discovery rescinds a previous discovery. Sciences of material facts and knowledge replace what proved to be wrong or inadequate with what is correct and adequate. Physical sciences are sciences of information, of specific answers to specific questions; they are sciences of causality, which makes their development a series of cancelations and replacements. In philosophy and idiographic sciences matters are different. The Battle of the Bulge could be reported historically from many points of view. The subjects of *morality* and *duty* could be discussed from the point-of-view of circumstances and principles as well as from the angle of obligation and freedom. *In the humanities we study the scientist's way of thinking and not just his thoughts.* Plato is still a basis for any philosophical study. Husserl is the first step to understanding Sartre's existentialism, and Hegel is torchlight to understanding Merleau Ponty. Thanks to Freud's remarkable ability to discern the wheat from the chaff we are able to extricate psychoanalysis from a nomothetic destiny that was awaiting it. We go back to *The Interpretation of Dreams* not to learn how to interpret dreams but to reexamine Freud's way of deducing the unconscious from the manifest of the psychical material; we will learn how Freud made the distinction between knowledge in psychoanalysis and the psychoanalytic way of thinking. Although discovering infantile sexuality upturned the theory of psychopathology in a radical way, Freud made the concept of *Trieb*—and not sexuality—the thing to last. Hence, psychoanalysis is not a science in the naïve meaning, which haunted psychoanalysis in North America for decades. Psychoanalysis is a way of thinking. Therefore, future psychoanalysis has to be the discovery of the psychoanalytic way of thinking to formulate intelligent questions for the other human sciences to get their answers. Analysis has access to many unknown aspects of the human mind that would put the discoveries of other human sciences in context and perspective. Learning about the new understandings of those aspects put psychoanalysis back on the map of the intellectual world.

NOTES

1. I know that the Canadian Psychoanalytic Society accepted non-clinical candidates in training (not members of the professions included in the health act), and they were left to their own means to practice analysis clinically. To my knowledge the A.Psyc.A. is opening membership to the analytic societies to non-clinical professionals. I am also told by some colleagues in other countries that some societies accept in training non-clinically educated candidates and for membership non-clinical professionals. In my judgment, this is done—up till now—mainly because of the falling numbers of applicants except in one society that I know, which did that out of conviction that psychoanalysis is more than a profession. However, that particular society got in trouble with the ministry of health in its country.

2. To begin with, there is a major difficulty with the main authors of the intersubjective theoretical framework, because of their dubious handling of the Freudian text. Sometimes they simply present him erroneously. In comparing their better system to Freud's Stolorow says (2011): "Trauma is viewed, not as an instinctual flooding of an ill-equipped Cartesian container, as Freud (1926) would have it, but as an unbearable affect" (7). Nevertheless, Freud said in the same text (1926d): "Anxiety never arises from repressed libido" (109). Freud is always depicted in Stolorow's mind as Cartesian. He states that "traditional Freudian theory is pervaded by the Cartesian 'myth of the isolated mind' . . . Descartes's (1641) philosophy bifurcated the subjective world into inner and outer regions, severed both mind from body and cognition from affect, reified and absolutized the resulting divisions, and pictured the mind as an objective entity" (3). Descartes is the first Western philosopher who came after the scholastic period. He influenced the whole group of Western philosophers who came after him; i.e., Freud did not choose Descartes but was a product of the Western philosophy that was Descartes heritage. Any educated reader of Western philosophy, which is the philosophy of the subject, recognizes that any approach taken to think about the subject had to be dualistic. Fichte built his arguments on differentiating between the I or the inner and the world, which was outer. Hegel's philosophy is the philosophy of the opposites which are interlinked in an endless chain of oppositions. Kant founded his philosophy on the opposition between the apriory and the aposteriori, and Leibniz on the experiential and the intentional. Schopenhauer made his duality between the primary and the derivative. Even Heidegger had his duality of authenticity and inauthenticity, and Kierkegaard in dealing with truth distinguished between subjective and objective truth and between Socratic knowledge and Christian knowledge. The same educated reader would see the same division in all the dualities between the subject and his world, conceptions and perceptions, between knowing and the unknown. Duality exists in Western culture for a simple reason: the first thing to do before embarking on discovering the subject, to start with proving first the certainty of the subject's existence, as Descartes did. Any educated reader of Western philosophy knows that *Cogito ergo sum* was not meant to separate the mind from the body but to empathize that one prove the existence of the other: *I would not be thinking if I am not*

there to think, and I am there because I am aware that I am thinking. I showed in my last book *Consciousness and the Aconscious in the Psychoanalytic Theory*, that Freud's theory is founded since his *Project* (1950a) on the organic link between body and consciousness.

3. This trend is still alive and strong. In December 2014 there was the following announcement in the *News Letter* of one of the best established institutions of psychoanalysis which also claims stringent adherence to the classical theory: "Dr. !!!! of the !!!!! Psychoanalytic Society and Institute is calling for 'A review of some of the Foundational Hypotheses Underlying Psychoanalytic Theory.' The hypotheses he suggested revisiting are repression, dynamic unconscious and psychosexual development evaluating them from today's vantage point of view." If we add those foundational hypotheses (hypotheses) to the rest of what was revised in the theory in the 1970s and 1980s what would be left of psychoanalysis is the suggested replacement hypotheses.

4. The young analyst was supposed to be a little reserved and distant (neutral); the older analysts were either so warm and fatherly, or haughty and pensive.

5. There is a major intellectual storm brewing now in neurology and philosophy regarding the concepts of consciousness, mind, the self (not the Kohutian one) and the unconscious.

6. The IPA published the requirements for qualification and admission to membership. There are three accredited models of training that qualify the candidate to membership: Eitington, the French, and Uruguayan.

7. In an interview with a six-year-old piano prodigy he explained how he plays so well: *I look at the notes and the music goes to my fingers.*

8. I have little solid knowledge about the philosophies of the Orient, and as far as I know the two early Middle Orient civilizations (Persia and lower Iraq) spread west and not east.

9. The *International Journal of Psycho-analysis, Journal of the American Psychoanalytic Association, Psychoanalytic Quarterly,* and *Psychoanalytic Psychology.*

10. French journals might have had more published works on training because in the 1950s there was the first split in the society, which was basically regarding training policies, followed by Lacan's challenging ideas both in theory and practice, culminating in "The Passe," and the issue of the status of the "training analyst" in the French Psychoanalytic Association.

11. The syllabus in the institute should concentrate on Freud's main works in four areas: the unconscious (the four main works on the unconscious between 1900 and 1905 and 1912), his work on *Trieb,* mental representations and narcissism (the revisions of 1915–1917), the works on the protocol of practice, and works on specific psychical phenomena like the Uncanny, Masochism, a child is beaten, etc. If those works are taught by a scholar of Freud, and major works added to them of other gifted analysts in the same areas, the foundation of the discovery of the theory of the mind would be established for building on without the need to go through the whole Freudian text (though this might entice people to do that later on). The syllabus could then be complimented by the basic arguments in the fields of linguistic studies, structural and social anthropology, logic and metaphysics, and child psychology. Neuropsychology, social psychology, and history of civilizations are very useful for a psychoanalytic viewpoint on the subject.

12. There is a popular YouTube video of two identical twins, 18 months of age at most, who were engaged in a very animated discussion with all the proper gestures that would accompany words, though they were not using any words of course but only their regular babble. They sounded convincingly as being in a true discussion and understanding and responding to each other. There were no sign that they were play-acting grown-ups roles except two fleeting smiles from one of them, which could suggest a momentary awareness of their funny act. Two of the many questions about their scene raises is how could they have discovered the linguistic meaning of talking to each before they learned how to speak? The other question is how did they develop the emotional content of that scene between them which was not expressing their own

emotions? Here is two toddlers who—for three minutes—related to each other supposedly telling each other something "very important" despite the absence of a stable sense of being. How much of failed psychoanalyses are similar to that child scene?

References

Alexander, F., and T. M. French. 1946. *Psychoanalytic therapy: Principles and application.* New York: The Ronald Press.

Alexander, F. 1963. *Fundamentals of psychoanalysis.* New York: Norton and Company.

American Psychoanalytic Association. 2002. *The American Psychoanalysts Quarterly Magazine.*

———. 2003. *The American Psychoanalysts Quarterly Magazine.*

———. 2004. *The American Psychoanalysts Quarterly Magazine.*

———. 2005. *The American Psychoanalysts Quarterly Magazine.*

———. 2006. *The American Psychoanalysts Quarterly Magazine.*

———. 2007. *The American Psychoanalysts Quarterly Magazine.*

———. 2010. *The American Psychoanalysts Quarterly Magazine.*

———. 2011. *The American Psychoanalysts Quarterly Magazine.*

———. 2012. *The American Psychoanalysts Quarterly Magazine.*

———. 2013. *The American Psychoanalysts Quarterly Magazine.*

———. 2014. *The American Psychoanalysts Quarterly Magazine.*

Anzieu, D. 1959. *L'auto-analyse, son role dans la dicoverte de la psychanalyse par Freud, sa function en psychanalyse.* Paris: Press Universitaires de France.

Arlow, J. 1977. Affect and the psychoanalytic situation. *International Journal of Psycho-Analysis* 58:157–70.

Arlow, J., and C. Brenner. 1964. *Psychoanalytic concepts and the structural theory.* New York: International Universities Press.

———. 1988. The future of psychoanalysis. *Psychoanalytic Quarterly* 57:1–14.

Barthes, R. 1996/1983. *A Barthes reader.* Trns. and Ed. S. Sontag. Harper Collins Canada ltd.

Basch, M. F. 1985. Some clinical and theoretical implications of infant research. *Psychoanalytic Inquiry* 5:509–16.

Bellak, L., M. Hurvich, and P. Crauford. 1969–1970. Psychological egos. *Psychoanalytic Review* 56D:526–42.

Bellak, I., and B. Meyers. 1975. Ego function assessment and analyzability. *Psychoanalytic Review* 2:413–27.

Beres, D., and E. Joseph. 1970. The concept of mental representation in psychoanalysis. *International Journal of Psychoanalysis* 51:1–8.

Bion, W. R. 1963. *Transformations.* London: Maresfield Reprints.

Boesky, D. 1983. The problem of mental representation in self and objet relations. *Psychoanalytic Quarterly* 52:564–83.

Bornstein, R. 2001. The impending death of psychoanalysis. *Psychoanalytic Psychology* 18:3–20.

———. 2007. Nomothetic psychoanalysis. *Psychoanalytic Psychology* 24:590–602.

Bowlby, J. 1981. Psychoanalysis as a natural science. *International Journal of Psycho-Analysis* 8:243–56.

Brenner, C. 1980. Metapsychology and the psychoanalytic theory. *Psychoanalytic Quarterly* 49:189–217.

———. 2000. Observations on some aspects of current psychoanalytic theories. *Psychoanalytic Quarterly* 69:597–632.

Breuer, J., and S. Freud. 1895. Studies on hysteria. *Standard Edition,* 2. London: The Hogarth Press and the Institute of Psycho-Analysis.

Bucci, W. 2000. The need for a "psychoanalytic psychology" in the cognitive science field. *Psychoanalytic Psychology* 17:203–24.
Calef, V. 1972. A report of the 4th the pre-congress training, Vienna 1971, to the International Psychoanalytic Congress. *International Journal of Psycho-Analysis* 53:37–44.
Cassirer, E. 1962/1944. *An essay on man: Introduction to a philosophy of human culture.* New Haven, CT: Yale University Press.
Cesio, F. 1995. *The crisis of psychoanalysis: An over view report of the House of Delegates Committee on the: Actual crisis of psychoanalysis: Challenges and Prospects.* Publication of The International Psychoanalytic Association.
Compton, A. 1981. On the psychoanalytic theory of instinctual drives. *The Psychoanalytic Quarterly* 50:190–218.
———. 1983. On the psychoanalytic theory of instinctual drives. *The Psychoanalytic Quarterly* 52:364–401.
Cooper, A. M. 1990. The future of psychoanalysis: Challenges and opportunities. *The Psychoanalytic Quarterly* 59::177–96.
Cornyetz, P. 1966. Classical psychoanalysis: The future of an idea. *Psychoanalytical Review* 53D:76–94.
Demos, V. 1985. The elusive infant. *Psychoanalytic Inquiry* 5:553–69.
Edelson, M. 1988. *Psychoanalysis: A theory in crisis.* Chicago, IL: University of Chicago Press.
Eisold, K. 1994. Intolerance to diversity in psychoanalytic institutions. *International Journal of Psycho-Analysis* 75:785–800.
———. 2003. The profession of psychoanalysis: Past failures and future possibilities. *Contemporary Psychoanalysis* 39:557–82.
———. 2007. The erosion of our profession. *Psychoanalytic Psychology* 24:1–9.
Eissler, K. R. 1969. Irreverent remarks about the present and the future of psychoanalysis. *International Journal of Psycho-Analysis* 50:461–71.
Ellman, C. S, and M. B. Moskowitz. 1980. An examination of some recent criticism of psychoanalytic "metapsychlogy." *Psychoanalic Quarterly* 49:631–62.
Erickson, E. 1952. The identity and the life cycle. *Psychoanalytic Issues* 1. New York: International Universities Press.
Eysenck, H. 1963. *Uses and abuses of psychology.* Baltimore, MD: Penguin.
Fayek, A. 2010. *The crisis in psychoanalysis: In search of a lost doctrine.* Austin, TX: Bridgeway Books.
———. 2014. *Consciousness and the aconscious in psychoanalytic theory.* Lanham, MD: Rowman and Littlefield.
Fenichel, O. 1953. *The collected papers of Otto Fenichel.* New York: Norton and Company.
Ferenczi, S. 1952. *Will therapy.* Baltimore, Johns Hopkins University Press.
———. 1980a. *Final contributions to the problems and methods of psychoanalysis.* New York: Brunner and Metzel.
———. 1980b. *Contributions to the problems and methods of psychoanalysis.* New York: Brunner and Metzel.
Firestein, S. 1978/2001. *Termination in psychoanalysis.* New York: International Universities Press.
Fliess, R. 1956. *Erogeneity and libido: Addenda to the theory of psychosexual development of the human.* New York: International University Press.
Flournoy, O. 1981. Reve et theorie. *Revue Francaise de Psychanalyse* XLV:227–47.
Freedman, A. 1974. The future of psychoanalysis as a profession. *Journal of the Academy of Psychoanalysis* 2:27–40.
Freedman, N. 1995. Interpretative summary: Four Perspectives on the "crisis." *The Actual Crisis of Psychoanalysis: Challenges and Perspectives.* International Psychoanalytic Association Publications.
Freud, S. 1894a. The neurospsychosis of defense. *Standard Edition* 3:41–61. London: The Hogarth Press and the Institute of Psycho-Analysis.

———. 1895. Letter (May 25). *The Complete Letters of Sigmund Freud to Wilhelm Flies,* (J. Masson, ed. and trans.). Cambridge, MA: The Belknap Press of Harvard University Press.

———. 1896b. Further remarks on the neuropsychosis of defense. *Standard Edition* 3:157–86. London: The Hogarth Press and the Institute of Psycho-Analysis.

———. 1897. Draft M Notes II (May 25). *The Complete Letters of Sigmund Freud to Wilhelm Flies* (J. Masson, ed. and trans.). Cambridge, MA: The Belknap Press of Harvard University Press.

———. 1898. Letter (March 10). *The Complete Letters of Sigmund Freud to Wilhelm Flies,* (J. Masson, ed. and trans.). Cambridge, MA: The Belknap Press of Harvard University Press.

———. 1900a. The interpretation of dreams. *Standard Edition,* 4–5. London: The Hogarth Press and the Institute of Psycho-Analysis.

———. 1901b. The psychopathology of everyday life. *Standard Edition,* 6. London: The Hogarth Press and the Institute of Psycho-Analysis.

———. 1905c. Jokes and their relations to the unconscious. *Standard Edition,* 8. London: The Hogarth Press and the Institute of Psycho-Analysis.

———. 1905d. Three essays to the theory of sexuality. *Standard Edition,* 7. London: The Hogarth Press and the Institute of Psycho-Analysis.

———. 1908b. Character and anal erotism. *Standard Edition* 9:167–76. London: The Hogarth Press and the Institute of Psycho-Analysis.

———. 1909b. Analysis of a phobia in a five-years-old boy. *Standard Edition* 10:1–150. London: The Hogarth Press and the Institute of Psycho-Analysis.

———. 1909c. Family romance. *Standard Edition* 11:219–30. London: The Hogarth Press and the Institute of Psycho-Analysis.

———. 1909d. Notes upon a case of obsessional neurosis. *Standard Edition,* 151–250. London: The Hogarth Press and the Institute of Psycho-Analysis.

———. 1910k. "Wild" psycho-analysis. *Standard Edition* 12:257–67. London: The Hogarth Press and the Institute of Psycho-Analysis.

———. 1911b. Formulation of the two principles of mental functioning. *Standard Edition* 12:213–26. London: The Hogarth Press and the Institute of Psycho-Analysis.

———. 1912b. The dynamics of transference. *Standard Edition* 12:97–108. London: The Hogarth Press and the Institute of Psycho-Analysis.

———. 1912c. Types of onset of neurosis. *Standard Edition* 12:227–38. London: The Hogarth Press and the Institute of Psycho-Analysis.

———. 1912g. Note on the unconscious. *Standard Edition* 12:257–67. London: The Hogarth Press and the Institute of Psycho-Analysis.

———. 1912–1913. Totem and taboo. *Standard Edition* 13:1–162. London: The Hogarth Press and the Institute of Psycho-Analysis.

———. 1913c. On the beginning of treatment (Further recommendations on the technique of psychoanalysis III). *Standard Edition* 12:121–44. London: The Hogarth Press and the Institute of Psycho-Analysis.

———. 1913j. The claims of psycho-analysis to scientific interest. *Standard Edition* 13:165–90.London: The Hogarth Press and the Institute of Psycho-Analysis.

———. 1914c. On narcissism: An introduction. *Standard Edition* 14:67–104.London: The Hogarth Press and the Institute of Psycho-Analysis.

———. 1915c. Instinct and their vicissitudes. *Standard Edition* 14:109–40. London: The Hogarth Press and the Institute of Psycho-Analysis.

———. 1915d. Repression. *Standard Edition* 14:141–58. London: The Hogarth Press and the Institute of psycho-analysis.

———. 1915e. The unconscious. *Standard Edition* 14:159–204. London: The Hogarth Press and the Institute of Psycho-Analysis.

———. 1916–1917. Introductory lecture on psycho-analysis. *Standard Edition,* 15–16. London: The Hogarth Press and the Institute of Psycho-Analysis.

———. 1917e. Mourning and melancholia. *Standard Edition* 14:237–59. London: The Hogarth Press and the Institute of Psycho-Analysis

———. 1920g. Beyond the pleasure principle. *Standard Edition* 18:1–64. London: The Hogarth Press and the Institute of Psycho-Analysis.
———. 1923a. Two encyclopedia article: (A) Psychoanalysis; (B) Libido theory. *Standard Edition, Standard Edition* 18:235–62. London: The Hogarth Press and the Institute of Psycho-Analysis.
———. 1923b). The ego and the id. *Standard Edition* 19:1–58. London: The Hogarth Press and the Institute of Psycho-Analysis.
———. 1926d. Inhibitions, symptoms, and anxiety. *Standard Edition* 20:75–176. London: The Hogarth Press and the Institute of Psycho-Analysis.
———. 1926e. The quest of lay analysis. *Standard Edition* 20:177–250. London: The Hogarth Press and the Institute of Psycho-Analysis
———. 1933a. New introductory lectures on psychoanalysis (lectures XXIX–XXXV). *Standard Edition* 22:159–204. London: The Hogarth Press and the Institute of Psycho-Analysis.
———. 1937c. Analysis terminable and interminable. *Standard Edition* 23:209–54. London: The Hogarth Press and the Institute of Psycho-Analysis.
———. 1940a. An outline of psycho-analysis. *Standard Edition* 23:139–207. London: The Hogarth Press and the Institute of Psycho-Analysis.
———. 1950a. Project for a scientific psychology. *Standard Edition* 23:139–207. London: The Hogarth Press and the Institute of Psycho-Analysis.
Gaddini, E. 1984. Changes in psychoanalytic patients up to the present time: Changes in analysts and their training. *Monograph Series* 4, Ed. R. Wallerstein. Publications of the International Psychoanalytic Association.
Gaensbauer, T. J. 1985. The relevance of infant research for psychoanalysis, *Psychoanalytic Inquiry* 5:517–30.
Gedo, J. 1999. *The evolution of psychoanalysis: Contemporary theory and practice.* New York: Other Press.
Gill, M. 1979. Topography and systems in psychoanalysis. *Psychological Issues, Monograph* 10. New York: International Universities press.
———. 1982. *Analysis of transference.* New York: International Universities Press.
Golgberg, A. 1978. *The psychology of the self: A casebook.* New York: International Universities Press.
Green, A. 1977. Conception of affect. *International Journal of Psychoanalysis* 58:129–57.
———. 1999. *The fabric of affect in psychoanalytic discourse* (A. Sheridan Trans.). London: Routledge.
———. 2000. The intrapsychic and intersubjectivity in psychoanalysis. *Psychoanalytic Quarterly* 69:1–40.
———. 2005. *Key ideas for a contemporary psychoanalysis: Misrecognition and recognition of the unconscious* (Andrew Weller, trans.). London: Routledge and The Institute of Psychoanalysis
Harari, Y. N. 2014. *A brief history of humankind: Sapiens.* Canada: Signal.
Hartmann, H. 1948. Comments on the psychoanalytic theory of instinctual drives. In *Essays on ego psychology: Selected problems in psychoanalytic theory.* New York: International Universities Press.
———. 1964. *Essays on ego psychology: Selected problems of psychoanalytic theory.* New York: International Universities Press.
Hauser, S. T. 2002. The future of psychoanalytic research: Turning points and new opportunities. *Journal of the American Psychoanalytic Association* 50:395–405.
Heiman, P. 1950. On counter transference. *International Journal of Psycho-Analysis* 31:343–58.
Holder, A. 1970. Instinct and drives. In H. Garma (ed.) *Basic psychoanalytic concepts on the theory of instinct,* Vol. III. London: The Hampstead Clinic Psychoanalytic Library.
Holt, R. 1965a. A review of some of Freud's biological assumptions and their influence on his theories. In N. S. Greenfield and W. C. Lewis (eds.), *Psychoanalysis and current biological thought,* 93–124. Madison: University of Wisconsin Press.

———. 1965b. Ego anatomy re-evaluated. *International Journal of Psycho-Analysis* 47:151–67.

———. 1976. Drive or wish: A reconstruction of the theory of psychoanalytic theory. In M. Gill and P. Holtzman (eds.), *Psychology versus metapsychology: Psychological essays in memory of G. Klein,* 159–97. *Psychological Issues, Monograph 36*. New York: International Universities Press.

Holtzman, P. S., and G. Aronson. 1992. Psychoanalysis and the neighboring sciences: Paradigms and opportunities. *Journal of the American Psychoanalytic Association* 40:63–88.

Home, J. 1966. The concept of the mind. *International Journal of Psycho-Analysis* 47:42–49.

Isaacs, S. 1948. The nature and function of phantasy. *The International Journal of Psycho-analysis* 29:73–97.

Johnson, S. M. 2003. *How history made the mind*. Chicago, IL: Open Court.

Jones, E. 1936. The future of psychoanalysis. *International Journal of Psycho-Analysis* 17:269–77.

———. 1957. *The life and work of Sigmund Freud.* London: The Hogarth Press.

Kernberg, O. 1967. Borderline personality disorders. *Journal of the American Psychoanalytic Association* 15:641–85.

———. 1996. Thirty methods to destroy the creativity of psychoanalytic candidates. *International Journal of Psychoanalysis* 77:1031–40.

———. 2007. The coming changes in psychoanalytic education: Part II. *International Journal of Psychoanalysis* 88:183–202.

King, P., and R. Steiner. 1991. *The Freud-Klein controversies 1941–1945.* London: Routledge.

Klein, G. 1976. *The psychoanalytic theory: An exploration of essentials.* New York: International Universities Press.

Klein, M. 1946. Note on some schizoid mechanisms. *International Journal of Psycho-Analysis* 27:99–110.

———. 1952. The origin of transference. *Internal Journal of Psycho-Analysis* 33:433–38.

Knap, P. H., S. Levin, R. H. McCarter, and E. Zetzel. 1960. Suitability for psychoanalysis: A review of one hundred supervised analytic cases. *Psychoanalytic Quarterly* 29:459–77.

Kohut, H. 1987. *Analysis of the self: An approach to psychoanalytic treatment of narcissistic disorders.* Chicago, IL: Chicago University Press.

Kubie, L. 1952. The independent institute on psychoanalytic technique. *Bulletin of The American Psychoanalytic Association* 8:205–8.

Lacan, J. 1977a. The mirror stage as a formative of the function of the I. In A. Sheridan (trans.), *Ecrits: A Selection.* New York: Norton and Company.

———. 1977b. The Freudian thing. In A. Sheridan (trans.), *Ecrits: A Selection.* New York: Norton and Company.

———. 1977c. The function and the field of speech and language in psychoanalysis. In A. Sheridan (trans.), *Ecrits: A Selection.* New York: Norton and Company.

Lakoff, G., and M. Johnson. 1980. *Metaphors we live by.* Chicago, IL: University of Chicago Press.

Laplanche, J. 1989. *New Foundation for psychoanalysis* (D. Macey, trans.). Oxford: Blackwell (original work published 1987.

———. 1992. Interpretation between determinism and hermeneutics: A restatement of the problem. *International Journal of Psychoanalysis* 73:429–46.

———. 1997. The theory of seduction and the problem of the other. *International Journal of Psycho-Analysis* 78:653–66.

Laplanche, J., and J. B. Pontalis. 1973. *The language of psychoanalysis* (D. N. Smith, trans.). New York: Norton and Company.

Levi-Strauss, C. 1974/1963. *Structural anthropology* (C. Jacobson, trans.). New York: Basic Books.

Limentani, A. 1974. The training analysis and the difficulties in the training situation. *International Journal of Psycho-Analysis* 55:71–77.
———. 1977. Affect in the psychoanalytic situation. *The International Journal of Psycho-analysis* 58:171–82.
Mackay, N. 1981. Melanie Klein's metapsychology: Phenomenological and mechanistic perspectives. *International Journal of Psycho-Analysis* 62:177–86.
Matte-Blanco, I. 1975. *The unconscious as infinite sets: An essay in bi-logic.* London: Duckworth.
Meissner, W. W. 1979a.Critique of concepts and therapy in active language approach to psychoanalysis. *International Journal of Psycho-Analysis* 60:291–310.
———. 1979b. Methodological critique of action language in psychoanalysis. *Journal of the American Psychoanalytic Association* 27:79–105.
Meltzer, R. 1978. *The Kleinian development, part 1: Freud's clinical development.* Perthshire: Clunie Press.
Michels, R. 1988. The future of psychoanalysis. *Psychoanalic Quarterly* 57:167–85.
Novey, S. 1958. The meaning of the concept of mental representation of the object, *Psychoanalytic Quarterly* 27:57–79.
Ogden, T. 1986. *The matrix of the mind: Object relations and the psychoanalytic dialogue.* Lanham, MD: Jason Aronson.
Orgel, S. 1990. The future of psychoanalysis. *Psychoanalytic Quarterly* 59:1–20.
PDM. 2008. *The Psychodynamic Diagnostic Manual.* Publication of the Alliance of Psychoanalytic Organizations.
Politzer, G. 1994. *Critique of the foundation of psychology* (A. Appry, trans.). Pittsburgh, PA: Duquesne University Press (original work published 1928.
Ponty, M. 2012. *The phenomenology of perception* (D. Landes, trans.). New York: Rutledge (original work published 1945.
Popper, K. R. 1974. *The philosophy of Karl Popper* (P. A. Schilpp, ed.). LaSalle, IL: Open Court.
Prelinger, E. 1972. Does psychoanalysis have a future in American psychology. *Psychoanalytic Quarterly* 41:90–103.
Pulver, S. 1971. Can affects be unconscious. *International Journal of Psycho-Analysis* 52:347–54.
Rangell, L. 1975. Psychoanalysis and the process of change: An essay on the past, present and future. *International Journal of Psychoanalysis* 56:87–98.
———. 1988. The future of psychoanalysis: The scientific crossroads. *Psychoanalytic Quarterly* 57:313–40.
———. 2000. Psychoanalysis in the millennium. *Psychoanalytic Psychology* 17:451–66
———. 2004. *My Life in Theory.* F. Busch, (Ed.), New York, Other Press.
Rank, O. 1952/1911. *The trauma of birth.* Eastford, TC: Martino Fine Books
———. 1968. *Will therapy and truth and reality* (J. Taft, trans.). Baltimore, MD: Johns Hopkins University Press.
Rappaport, D. 1951. The conceptual model of psychoanalysis. In Knight and Friedman (eds.). *Psychoanalytic psychology and psychology, clinical and theoretical papers.* New York: International University Press.
Rappaport, D., and M. Gill. 1959. The points of view and assumptions of metapsychology. *The International Journal of Psychoanalysis* 40:153–62.
Reich, W. 1945. *Character analysis.* New York: Organ Institute Press.
Reisner, S. 1999. Freud and psychoanalysis: Into the 21st century. *Journal of the American Psychoanalytic Association* 47:1037–60.
Richards, A. D. 1990. The future of psychoanalysis: The past, present, and future of psychoanalytic theory. *Psychoanalytic Quarterly* 59:347–69.
Richards, A. D., and A. Lynch. 2008. The identity of psychoanalysis and psychoanalysts. *Psychoanalytic Psychology* 25:203–19.
Ricoeur, P. 1970. *Freud and philosophy: An essay on interpretation* (D. Savage, trans.). New Haven, CT: Yale University Press.

Rosenblatt, A., and J. Thickstun. 1997. *Modern psychoanalytic concepts in general psychology, psychlogical issues, Monograph 63/63*. New York: International Universities Press.

Royden, C., and M. D. Astley. 1974. Psychoanalysis: The future. *Journal of the American Psychoanalytic Association* 22:83–96.

Rubinstein, B. 1997. Psychoanalysis and the philosophy of science. In R. Holt (ed.), *Psychological Issue: Monograph 62/63*. New York: International Universities Press.

Safouan, M. 1983. *Pleasure and being*, London: MacMillan Press.

Sandler, J., and B. Rozenblatt. 1962. The concept of representational world. *The Psychoanalytic Study of the Child* 17:128–45.

Sapir, E. 2008/1939. *Language: An introduction to the study of speech* (Amazon Kindle Edition).

Saussure de, F. 1998/1912. *Course in general linguistics* (C. Bally and A.Schehaye, eds.; R. Harris, trans.), Chicago, IL: Open Court.

Schachter, J. 2005. Contemporary American psychoanalysis: A profession? Increasing the role of research in psychoanalysis. *Psychoanalytic Psychology* 22:473–92.

Schafer, R. 1976. *A new language for psychoanalysis*. New Haven, CT: Yale University Press.

Spillius, E. B. 1992. On the concept pf phantasy. Paper presented to C.P.S. Montral.

Spruiell, V. 1989. The self and the ego. *Psychoanalytic Quarterly* 50:319–44.

Stechler, G. 1985. The study of infants engenders systemic thinking. *Psychoanal Inquiry* 5:531–41.

Stechler, G., and A. Kaplan. 1980. The development of the self: A psychoanalytic perspective. *The Psychoanalytic Study of the Child* 35:85–105.

Stekle, W., and L. London. 1933. The future of psychoanalysis. *Psychoanalytic Review* 20:327–33.

Stolorow, R. 2011. From mind to world, from drive to affectivity: A phenomenological-conceptualist psychoanalytic perspective, Attachment. *New Directions in Psychotherapy and Relational Psychoanalysis* 5:1–14.

Stolorow, R., G. Atwood, and D. Orang. 2002. *Worlds of experience: Interweaving philosophical and clinical dimensions in psychoanalysis*. New York: Basic Books.

Vygotsky, L., and A. Kozalin. 1986. *Thought and language*, revised and edited by A. Kozalin. Cambridge: The Massachusetts Institute of Tecnology.

Wallerstein, R. 1986. *Forty-two lives in treatment*. New York: Guilford.

———. 1988. One psychoanalysis or many? *The International Journal of Psychoanalysis* 69:5–21.

———. 1990. Psychoanalysis: The common grounds. *International Journal of Psychoanalysis* 71:3–20.

———. 2005. Will psychoanalytic pluralism be an enduring state of the discipline? *International Journal of Psychoanalysis* 86:623–26.

Wallerstein, R. S., and E. M. Weinshel. 1989. The future of psychoanalysis. *Psychoanalytic Quarterly* 58:341–73.

Westen, D. 1999. The scientific status of unconscious processes: Is Freud really dead? *Journal of the American Psychoanalytic Association* 47:1061–106.

Windelband, W. 2001/1893. *A history of philosophy: With special reference to the formation and development of its problems and conceptions* (J.Tufts, trans.). Toronto: The Macmillan Company of Canada.

Winnicott, D. 1955. Clinical variations of transference. In *Collected papers: Through pediatrics to psychoanalysis*. New York: Basic Books.

Index

About the Author

Ahmed Fayek is a retired clinical psychologist and a training and supervising psychoanalyst. He graduated with a PhD from Ein-Shams University in Cairo in 1962, and worked in academia from 1959–1970. He had unaccredited psychoanalytic training in Egypt. When he moved to Canada he had a second accredited training in the Canadian Psychoanalytic Institute and participated in training and supervising candidates and junior psychoanalysts until 2000. In Canada he was the psychologist-in-chief at St. Mary's Hospital in Montreal and the director of psychology at the Royal Ottawa Hospital.